Barcelona
Style

Barcelona
Style

Publisher: **Paco Asensio**

Text: **Lluís Tolosa and Cristina Montes**

Coordination and captions: **Susana González**

Translation: **Harry Paul**

Proofreading: **Julie King**

Art Director: **Mireia Casanovas Soley**

Layout: **Emma Termes Parera**

Copyright for the international edition:

© **Kliczkowski Publisher-A Asppan S.L.**

Fundición, 15. Polígono Industrial Sta. Ana

Rivas-Vaciamadrid. 28529 Madrid

Tel.: +34 91 666 50 01

Fax: +34 91 301 26 83

asppan@asppan.com

www.onlybook.com

ISBN: **84-89439-57-5**

D.L.: **B-24.005/2001**

Editorial project:

LOFT Publications

Domènec, 9 2-2

08012 Barcelona. Spain

Tel.: +34 93 218 30 99

Fax: +34 93 237 00 60

e-mail: loft@loftpublications.com

www.loftpublications.com

Printing:

Indústrias Gráficas Ferré Olsina. Barcelona

June 2001

Barcelona
Style

S unny winter days are ideal for sitting on the terrace of Café Zurich in Plaça Catalunya. Clear, blue skies are common during Barcelona's winter season, creating the perfect moment to enjoy a drink and soak in the Mediterranean sun. However, Plaça Catalunya is also the city's cosmopolitan centre and a prime spot to people-watch and begin to understand Barcelona. Tourists mingle with street musicians, retirees with time on their hands, teenagers and pretty young people out to see and be seen, aware that nowhere else in Barcelona are they going to catch so many admiring looks. The scene is constantly changing. The people sitting at the café tables watch the passers by and vice-versa.

The variety in Barcelona is not only reflected in the visitors and inhabitants. Looking around Plaça Catalunya one can observe many different architectural trends. The Café Zurich is part of El Triàngle shopping mall, a modern, graceful construction built using new construction techniques. In contrast, across the square, the solid, classic buildings of the Fifties and Sixties recall the con-

servatism of design during Franco's dictatorship. The only modernist building in the square is located on the corner diagonally opposite the café, on Ronda Sant Pere. Its Gothic gargoyles and ornamental flowers are echoed in other buildings around the city.

Whether by chance or by design, Plaça Catalunya is a fair representation of the varied styles found in Barcelona. Faithful to the history and the development of the city, this book will enable the reader to experience the sensations of visiting the sights, revealing their mysteries and unveiling the most stimulating places. Barcelona's charm will enthrall you.

History

1. The archaeological remains from the Roman period reflect of the customs and economic prosperity of the Romans.

2. The Carrer del Bisbe, which begins in Plaça Nova, was the Roman *decumanus*. Not far away, you find Carrer Ferran, which took over from the *cardo*.

*C*ity wall is a physical reflection of how ways of life have changed in the city throughout history. The wall has always seemed to be holding back the city's expansion. First, there was the Roman wall that protected a small area as it became increasingly prosperous, trade flourished and the life grew more hectic. In Medieval times, the wall moved outwards but it always remained one step behind the increase in the population and in the industrial and commercial activity, causing the living conditions within its confines to become unsustainable. Epidemics spread easily and ravaged the population.

However, since Barcelona was a military stronghold, the central government in Madrid was not prepared to give in to the popular clamour calling for its demolition. Looking at Barcelona today, it is hard to believe that its Medieval walls were knocked down only in 1854, less than 150 years ago. But when they did come down, the city then began to expand following the grid plan of urban designer Ildenfons Cerdà, which is still visible in the Eixample district (which literally means "to widen"). As the city expanded, it absorbed the villages around the old city, like Gràcia, Sant Andreu, Sants and Sarrià, all of which today are now neighbourhoods within Barcelona.

Since the city walls were torn down, Barcelona has grown and changed. Three key events catapulted the city forward: two expositions and the Olympic Games.

Barcino, the Roman city

The centre of the ancient Roman cities was the *forum*, the square in which all meetings of public interest were held. This place, of capital importance in the city's life, had to be located in the heart of the city and had to represent the splendour of the Roman empire.

Two thousand years after its foundation, Barcelona still conserves some of its Roman cultural remains. If you stand in what is today **Plaça Nova**, in front of the round columns of the old city gate, on your left, you can see the remains of one of the arches that held up the aqueduct. Before you lies the **Carrer del Bisbe**, which back in Roman times was one of the principal

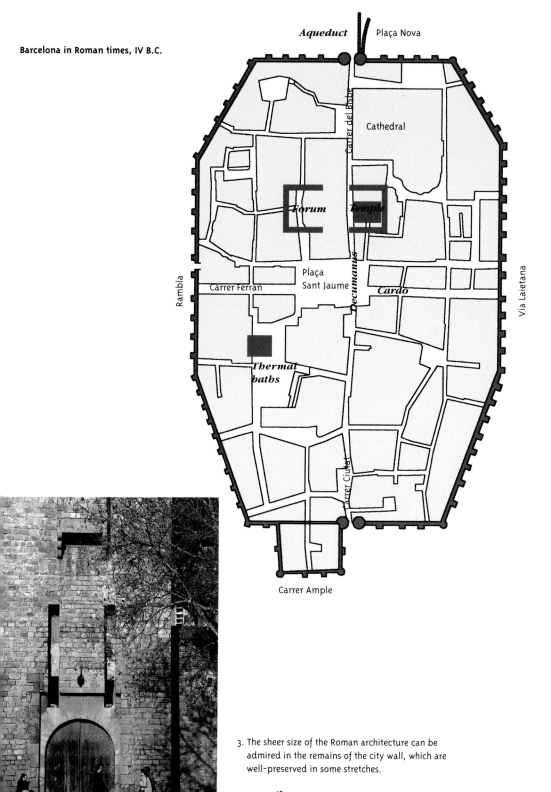

Barcelona in Roman times, IV B.C.

Aqueduct Plaça Nova

Carrer del Bisbe

Cathedral

Forum *Temple*

Rambla

Carrer Ferran

Plaça
Sant Jaume

Decumanus

Cardo

Via Laietana

*Thermal
baths*

Carrer Ciutat

Carrer Ample

3. The sheer size of the Roman architecture can be
admired in the remains of the city wall, which are
well-preserved in some stretches.

3

Carrer Fontanella

Ronda Sant Pere

Passeig Lluís Companys

3

11

9

10

8

Passeig Colom

MEDITERRANEAN SEA

Barcelona in the 15th century
1. Library of Catalonia
   (former hospital of
   Santa Creu)
2. Boqueria market
3. Cathedral of Barcelona
4. Plaça Sant Jaume
5. Church of Santa Maria del Pi
6. Plaça Reial
7. Church of Santa Ana
8. Church of Santa Maria
   del Mar
9. Convent of San Agustín
10. Born market
11. Santa Caterina market

thoroughfares of the city. Today, the core of the old city is still a maze of narrow streets amongst which you can find magnificent medieval buildings. In the middle is the **Plaça Sant Jaume,** the old Roman forum into which the two main streets of the Roman city converged, the *cardo* and the *decumanus*.

It is curious to think that certain ways of doing things have remained the same since the Romans were in power. Evidence of this is the Roman *forum*, which is still the place where most of demonstrations and public celebrations take place. For example Barcelona FC and their fans come here when they win a trophy. However, the crowds do not always come to cheer: political demonstrations also take place here. While the public chants and waves banners, the politicians normally steer clear of the balconies and stay inside the imposing buildings on either side of the square, the headquarters of the Ajuntament de Barcelona (City Hall) and the Generalitat de Catalunya (the Catalan national goverment). The two buildings face each other across the square, physically depicting how their political colours have clashed since the restoration of democracy in the Seventies.

If you want to travel back in time and see what life was like in the ancient city of Barcino, there is no better place to visit than the **Museu d'Història de la Ciutat,** in the Plaça del Rei.

The city during the Middle Ages

On a map of Barcelona today, the three different walls which the city grew into and out of are still evident. The first, the Roman wall, was built in the 1st century B.C., and then reconstructed several times up to the end of the 4th century B.C. The other two walls did not go up until the Middle Ages: the first between the 13th and 15th centuries, and the second between the 14th and 15th centuries. Today they form a circular route around what was the old city: **Ronda Sant Pau, Ronda Sant Antoni, Carrer Pelai, Ronda Sant Pere, Passeig Lluís Companys, Avinguda Marquès d'Argentera, Passeig Colom, Avinguda Paral·lel** and finally the **Rambla,** marking a frontier between the ordered world inside the city walls and the agricultural fields outside.

However, it was inside the city walls that the character of Barcelona began to take shape. The invasion of the Moors, who had overrun nearly all the Iberian Peninsula, reached as far as Barcelona, but they were driven back by the arrival on the scene of the troops of the French King Louis I, the Pious. In recog-

4. The origins of the cathedral go back to the Roman basilica with its three naves, originally Visigoth but destroyed by Al-Mansur in the year 925. In 1298, a new construction was started. Its façade was left unfinished and it was not completed until the 19th century when Josep Oriol Mestres and August Font accepted the charge of finishing it according to the 15th century drawings.

nition of his help, the people of Barcelona accepted becoming part of the Charlemagne empire known as the Spanish March. Frankish sovereignty over Barcelona was nominal, but afforded the people the status of Freemen and permitted them to have their own government despite the prevailing feudal system.

It was at this time that Barcelona became known as the Ciutat Condal because of the appointment of a count to control the city. At first the counts were mostly foreign, but as time went by the Frankish influence faded and the city became an independent administrative area.

Barcelona enjoyed a privileged position for it had sufficient liberty to strive to develop as a community at a time when the rest of the Iberian peninsula was struggling to push back the Muslims. The city was able to take advantage of the Frankish influence to develop trade relations while strengthening control of its domains with a double strategy. The first was to fight back against the Arabs, especially under Jaume I the Conqueror, and the second was to take advantage of the astute marriage of Count Ramon Berenguer IV of Barcelona to Petronila, queen of Aragon, after which Catalonia and Aragon were united under the same ruler. This kingdom stretched from Valencia, across the River Ebro and up to Provence, and even across the sea to Majorca and other points around the western Mediterranean.

The resulting period of prosperity and tranquillity was an ideal opportunity for new communities to grow up outside the city walls. One example was the neighbourhood around the **church of Pi**, in the square of the same name, besides which simple peasant folk lived and grew vegetables. Still standing today, the church of **Santa Maria del Mar** became the centre of a neighbourhood populated by merchants, sailors, fishermen and shipowners. The bustling activity attracted traders from Genoa, Greece, Egypt and other ports. The merchants, too, set up delegations over the sea, extending the country's influence.

During the 13th century, all this expansion meant that once again **Barcelona** was bursting at the seams and a new wall was necessary. The main stretch of the new construction ran along what today is the Rambla promenade, one of the most famous avenues in the world. Back in the Middle Ages the day labourers would gather on this street at dawn waiting to be hired. It was also the site of the livestock and agriculture market.

5

5. The Palau de la Generalitat has been the site of the Catalan government since 1403. The façade dates to the end of the 16th century and includes sculptures of the three deputies who ordered its construction, and the cross of Sant Jordi, the symbol of the institution.

Since wars could flare up quickly, a third wall was soon erected to protect the new crop lands and to ensure self-sufficiency in case of attack. The walled protection extended to the **Avinguda Paral·lel**. Today all that remains is the fort of **Santa Madrona**. Thus, at the end of the 15th century, the city and its crop land was clearly defined within the two walled rings, both of them sharing the stretch along the Rambla.

Social organisation

These walls protected a city which was advanced due to two main reasons. On one hand, there was the legal organisation based on a written body of law, the Usatges, which from the 13th century onwards established the rights and liberties granted by the Frank kings and successively confirmed by the counts of Barcelona and applicable to all Catalonia and Majorca. It has been said that this document was the first constitution of any European country. The other positive factor spurring on the city's development was the degree of civil participation in decision making. Executive authority was entrusted to a council of five who were accountable before a larger Consell de Cent, or council of one hundred.

This spirit favouring the participation of the citizens carried over to the maintenance and defence of the city walls. Until the 19th century all adult males (except priests and monks) were obliged to play their part, often backed up by the strong guild organisation in the woollen industry across Catalonia.

In 1714, this civilian heroism reached its peak. In the War of Spanish Succession the forces of Felipe V lay siege to the city with an army of 40,000 soldiers. Barcelona was completely subjugated; 5,000 armed guildsmen were no match for them and when the city fell, Felipe V did away with the Catalan constitution, as well as all forms of local government and autonomy.

The date of this defeat, the 11th of September, is a national holiday in Catalonia, known as the Diada. It is a peaceful celebration which commemorates the loss of a federal system, a setback for civil rights and the imposition of an absolute monarchy. With the war out of the way, Felipe V started confiscating land, withdrawing titles and privileges. The settling of old scores forced some people into exile. The whole sad process ended up in 1716 with a decree that dismantled all Catalan institutions and forbid the use of the Catalan language, imposing Spanish as the unique official language.

The repression of the Catalan identity was physically

6. The Plaça de l'Arc de Triomf, at the beginning of Passeig Lluís Companys, formed an impressive entrance to the Universal Exposition of 1888. The broad walkway changed its name to Passeig dels Til·lers and led to the site of the show.

7. The Castell dels Tres Dracs, today the Museu de Zoologia, was built in 1888 based on a project by Domènech i Montaner. It was to house the café-cum-restaurant of the exposition but the plan was never carried out.

8. The Hivernacle is a magnificent iron and metal building that served as a greenhouse during the expo. In 1985 it was rescued from its run-down state and put to use for temporary exhibitions and musical performances.

symbolised on both edges of the city. On top of Montjuïc, mountain stood the **castle** overlooking the city below. On the other side of the city, 1,200 houses were razed to the ground to make way for the **Ciutadella** (a fortress and military prison). Not one owner was compensated, and the men who had helped to hold out against the siege were stripped of their professional status and obliged to shovel away the debris.

Strides towards a modern city

Renowned for their business acumen, the Catalans have always relied on industry and commerce to spur on the growth of Barcelona. Three historic events provided the opportunity to strengthen the economy and modernise the city. The first of these events was the Universal Exposition of 1888; the second was the International Exposition of 1929, and the third were the Olympic Games of 1992. On these three occasions, Barcelona has revived the city and realised the dreams of many years.

The Industrial Revolution

It was the process of industrialisation that spurred on economic development. A society was born that was based on the ideological and political profiles of the new emerging classes: the bourgeoisie and the proletariat. Both helped shape the city's new personality: the proletariat for their uprisings and social demands, and the bourgeoisie as the class behind the urban, political and cultural renovation of Catalonia and its capital, Barcelona.

The factories with their steam powered machines were installed in Barcelona and the houses for the workers were built around them. The engine of the Catalan economy was cotton, which gave impetus to other major industries like machines and metals. In absolute terms Catalonia was the fourth cotton producer in Europe, but in per capita production it was the leader.

Barcelona's first textile factory went into operation in 1832 and the city became the principal producer of a cotton fabric known as "indianas", on which the pattern was only printed on one side. Other factories soon sprang up, changing the urban landscape and invigorating the economy to such an extent that by 1900 nearly half of Spain's imports came via Catalonia. In 1848 the first railway line in Spain came into service between Mataró and Barcelona.

Two factors, however, shaped Barcelona's industrial evolution. The first was the need to import coal from

9, 10, 11. Images of Plaça Catalunya, the Portal de l'Àngel and the port of Barcelona in 1905.

Great Britain, which had an effect all down the supply chain. The second factor was the squalid living conditions of the workers around the factories and the consequent social unrest.

Both of these problems were solved by moving the factories outside of the city, especially to the land alongside the River Llobregat where they could exploit hydraulic power. Workers colonies were set up around the companies, following the traditional English style which included a church, the possibility of health care and other amenities tantamount to a better standard of living.

This industrial heritage is well-conserved both in Barcelona and in Catalonia. In the 1990's many industrial estates were converted into pleasant neighbourhoods, where the past is symbolised by chimneys wich stand among modern apartment buildings.

The most enjoyable way of seeing how things were one hundred years ago when the euphoria pushed industry forward is to visit the **Museu de la Ciència i la Tècnica de Catalunya**, in Terrassa. If you want to see the creative atmosphere generated during this era, take a stroll along **Passeig de Gràcia** where you can admire the modernist facades of the **Pedrera**, the **Casa Amatller**, the **Casa Batlló**, and other houses built by the Catalan bourgeoisie.

The Universal Exposition of 1888

Holding this exposition in Barcelona fittingly showed to what extent the city had come to occupy a privileged economic and cultural position in Europe. This wealth had rekindled the demands of the Catalans for more autonomy, and the presence of the **Ciutadella** was an insult to the people of the city. In 1869 its stout walls were demolished and the land was converted into the delightful park it is today. The old arsenal of the Ciutadella houses the Parlament de Catalunya.

Once the Ciutadella was out of the way, with all of its military overtones, the most prestigious architects of that time started to work on a majestic complex in which to hold the exposition.

The **Arc de Triomf** majestically marked the entrance to the site, and led into a wide mall and the exposition area. This green open space is still preserved today and is now called Passeig Lluís Companys. The works also included **Passeig Colom** and a new port, known today as **Moll de la Fusta**, which stretched to the **Portal de la Pau** where the statue of Christopher Columbus was erected.

12. The Palau Nacional de Montjuïc, built for the grand ceremonies of the International Exposition of 1929, today houses the Museu Nacional d'Art de Catalunya, a complete collection of works from the 11th century through to the end of the 20th century.

The outside of the exposition halls, the Rambla and the path leading up to the halls were decked out for the gala. Electric street lighting was used in Barcelona for the first time, and for a trip around the port, one could hire a **Golondrina** or swarrow boat, which is still possible today.

The International Exposition of 1929

The Universal Exposition of 1888 was visited by at least two million people. Such success meant that no sooner had it closed its doors than the people of Barcelona began to talk about the need to repeat the experience. Political agreements and ambitiousness of the urban plans delayed this aspiration, but it was the military pronouncement of General Primo de Rivera (1923) that halted the project for good.

By now, Barcelona was the most important industrial city in Spain and one of the most populated cities around the Mediterranean. It had a subway system, the streets were paved, the drainage and water supply worked well and there was a good electricity network.

However, such improvements in the infrastructure did not mean that Barcelona had forgotten about its history. 1888 brought the end of the military Ciutadella and the unwelcome external influence it symbolised, so the International Exposition of 1929 was the chance to turn **Montjuïc**, with the castle on top, into a relaxing park for the inhabitants to enjoy, rather than just a hill with a fortress at the top. The urban reform did not finish here. **Plaça Espanya** was tarmaced and a massive site for trade fairs and shows was constructed. Its entrance was marked by two high Venetian towers, leading up to the steps to the Palau Nacional, the authentic heart of the celebration. The most innovative aspect, however, was the **Magical Fountain** which combined light and water. The city council still puts on the show, and has added music.

The area conserves the spirit of that era since it now serves as the location of various national and international trade fairs and has maintained its original landscaped zone.

The Dictatorship

Unfortunately, this period of cultural effervescence was soon to be cut short by the tragic outbreak of the Spanish Civil War (1936-1939). The Nationalists' victory under Franco resulted in a loss of autonomy and the repression, once again, of Catalan nationalism.

13. Plaça Espanya was tarmaced in 1929 in preparation for the International Exposition.
In the centre there is a fountain designed by the architect Josep Maria Jujol, a disciple of Gaudí. It includes marble and bronze statues by Miquel Blay.

After the war, Spain was a country divided into winners and losers. Consequently, opportunities for development were missed as Spain became isolated, and excluded from international organisations like the United Nations. However, beginning in 1950, Spain established itself as a great place for vacations and the economy shifted up a gear, generating immigration towards Catalonia to fill vacancies in factories. In general, the immigrants from the rest of Spain settled in towns around the edge of Barcelona.

The death of General Franco in 1975 was followed by the establishment of democratic rule. The agreements signed with the central government in Madrid detailed new areas for self-government under the Generalitat and gave rise to a wide range of developments in Barcelona as the city saw the opportunity to catch up with the rest of Europe.

The 1992 Olympic Games

The whole process of competing for the Olympic nomination, getting the city ready and actually hosting the games turned the Catalan capital into a buzz of activity. The enthusiasm was especially noticeable among the young people who participated as volunteers in a whole host of activities. Barcelona was very much in fashion and its design skills were advertised all over the world, with the Olympic mascot designed by Mariscal as the symbol. As so many Olympic installations had to be built, the city planners seized the chance to open up the city to the sea and recover the **beaches**. The **Olympic Port** (Port Olímpic) and the **Olympic Village** (Vila Olímpica) were built close together. Barcelona began to feel even more Mediterranean. The Ronda beltway around the city came into service in an attempt to ease the downtown traffic congestion.

After the intense preparations, the great moment came in the summer of 1992 when the Opening Ceremony was held, a spectacle of light, colours and imagination which was praised world-wide. Barcelona had recovered its self-confidence and hope for the future, projecting an image of a city enriched by design and with an excellent quality of life. Barcelona soon became a "must see" destination for tourists getting away for a short break or on their way to beaches along the Mediterranean coast. Magnificent hotels were built to cater for the

14. The Estadi Olímpic, when built in 1929 as part of the infrastructure for the International Exposition, was the second biggest stadium in the world. From 1985 onwards it was revamped in the run up to the Olympic Games, brought up to current safety standards and fitted out with modern facilities. Its capacity is now 60,000 spectators.

demand. While all this was going on, forward looking people began to look for the next opportunity to
host an international event: the Universal Cultural
Forum of 2004.

The Universal Cultural Forum

Barcelona is getting ready for Universal Cultural Forum
of 2004, which will mostly take place around
the area where the Besòs river runs into the
sea. There is hope that its impact will be as
significant as the expositions and the
Olympic Games.

Aimed at bringing diverse cultures together,
there are three inter-related ideas behind
the program of events: diversity, sustain-
able development and peace. Debates will
take place, and there will be expositions and
a festival of arts from all over the world.
Reflection will be encouraged alongside
dialogue and entertainment, all against a backdrop
of people learning to share life.

This international meeting is another opportunity to
give the city an urban makeover. New buildings are
being constructed for the main events by the mouth
of the Besòs river, where Avinguda Diagonal meets
the sea. This zone was considered as a possibility for
the International Exposition of 1929. However, it was
not selected and today is rather run down. When the
rehabilitation works are finished, Barcelona will
have gained another residential and tourist neighbourhood in line with the policy of ensuring that
these type of events spread improvements over all
the city. Of course, pre-existing cultural facilities
will also play a part in the program.

15. The German Pavilion for 1929 was commissioned to the prestigious architect Mies Van der Rohe. The constructions built for the Exposition were normally intended to be short-lived, but Van der Rohe's project was so acclaimed by critics and public alike that the authorities decided to maintain it. Over the years, it has become one of architectural icons of the city.

Barcelona, sky, sea and mountain

Barcelona, a small city compared with other European metropolitan areas, is still marked by the urban reform plan inspired by the Olympic Games. The city lies on a plain confined by the Besòs river and the Llobregat river, the rocky outcrop of Montjuïc and the mountains.

Life in Barcelona is affected by the geographical limits, which tend to make it a rather congested urban area. The street system is characterised by the grid layout in the central Eixample district. Some streets go up and others go across as the city, which begins by the sea and runs up to the foot of the mountains.

Thinking in terms of the sea and mountain side makes it easy to orient oneself in Barcelona. Addresses and how to get there always tend to be defined by being on either the "sea" side or the "mountain" side of a street. Alternatively, vertical streets on the map are defined as on "Llobregat side", to the west, or "Besòs side", to the east.

In terms of neighbourhoods, the people who live close to the mountain, in the upper part of the city, tend to enjoy a higher standard of living. Barcelona slopes upwards and the social class follows suit. The wide streets at the foot of **Mount Tibidabo** were traditionally the out-of-town holiday homes of the Catalan bourgeoisie after the Industrial Revolution. Although the city spread upwards over time the sense of prosperity has been conserved. There are fine mansions, beautiful parks and the most expensive private schools. The neighbourhood is especially popular among advertising companies who have turned some of the grand houses into their headquarters.

Olympic Barcelona

The makeover of 1992 is still noticeable in Barcelona today. That year represented a profound change for the city, especially the regaining of contact with the beaches — previously too close to the traditionally industrial Icària zone. For the first time in many years, the people of Barcelona had the chance to stroll along the seafront. Until the year 1986, when Juan Antonio Samaranch, the Catalan President of the International Olympic Committee, pronounced the words "a la ville de Barcelone", unleashing the joyous reaction of Catalans, Barcelona had strangely turned its back on the Mediterranean. Barcelona had been given four years to get ready for the great event and the sea was going to play a key role in the reformation.

To take in the beauty of the new Barcelona born out of the Olympic Games you should head to **Montjuïc**, the **Palau Sant Jordi**, the renovated **Estadi Olímpic** and, above all, the telecommunications tower designed by the architect **Santiago Calatrava**. It rises up out of the top of Montjuïc mountain near the Olympic stadium.

Another architectural reference point is the Collserola tower, designed by the Norman Foster. Minimalist and modern, this sleek tower twinkles over the city at night from Mount Tibidabo. The triangle of exhilarating landmarks scraping the sky is completed on the waterfront by the twin towers of the **Hotel Arts**, designed collectively by a group of American architects, and the **Torre Mapfre**, an office building created by Iñigo Ortiz and Enrique León. However, the **Vila Olímpica** is surely the most ambitious and significant architectural legacy of the Games. It is a self-sufficient microcosmos inside the city, a symbol of the success of the Barcelona games and the spirit with which they were approached.

1. The vitrified ceramic exterior of Palau Sant Jordi, designed by Arata Isozaki, stands on the ground like an alien object. Inside, however, recessed lights that spray light across the immense metal structure invert this sensation.

2. Opened in 1929 for the International Exposition, the Montjuïc stadium became Olympic in 1992 and other installations were built around it to host the Games. Its reconstruction only preserved the original façade.
3. Santiago Calatrava designed a telecommunications tower with a shaft slanted to coincide with the summer solstice in Barcelona. Today, it is no longer used, but remains a decorative element on the Barcelona skyline.

Saunter around the **Port Olímpic** — where the yachts are moored — and **Maremàgnum**, a shopping mall, to enjoy seafront bars and terraces. There is wide range entertainment for the entire family and all ages. On sunny days the sidewalk is full of people on bicycles, roller skates and pushing strollers enjoying the sea air.
And to round off the possibilities there are five kilometres of well maintained beaches with surprisingly clean water.

4. Along the seafront the contrast between traditional architecture and modern designs is very evident. The monument to Columbus in front of this building now owned by the Port Authorities, originally built as the most luxurious hotel for the Exposition of 1888, and the triangle lampposts seen in the picture are a fine illustration of how to blend old and new.

5. In 1996 City Hall named a square in honour of the volunteers who enabled the Olympic dream to be turned into a reality. This monument, the Marc Escultura — by Robert Llimós — , was erected in the Plaça dels Voluntaris.

6. The glass structure of the Torre Mapfre and the metal cladding of the Hotel Arts catch the eye from any high point across the city, advertising the way Barcelona has regained contact with the seafront.

Blue Barcelona

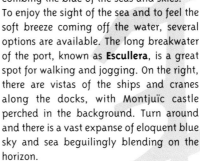

U p until 1992, only the fisherman's neighbourhood of **Barceloneta** was closely related to the sea. Everyday boats come in from the Mediterranean and auction off their catch along the wharves at the end of **Passeig Joan de Borbó**. However, refomations to the city have returned great stretches of the waterfront to Barcelona, offering numerous views combing the blue of the seas and skies.

To enjoy the sight of the sea and to feel the soft breeze coming off the water, several options are available. The long breakwater of the port, known as **Escullera**, is a great spot for walking and jogging. On the right, there are vistas of the ships and cranes along the docks, with Montjuïc castle perched in the background. Turn around and there is a vast expanse of eloquent blue sky and sea beguilingly blending on the horizon.

Although you will only have water on one side, another possibility is to stroll along **Moll de la Fusta** until you come to the terraces of the bars and restaurants by **Palau de Mar**. Here, you can have breakfast, lunch or dinner with a view of ship's sails. If you still feel energetic, keep going towards the beaches by the Olympic Port.

As for the sky, it is often blue in Barcelona, but some days the intense clarity and reflection off the water makes it seem as if it is playing a trick on your eyes. Spend a day like this at the **Mirador del Tibidabo** or the observation post of **Torre de Collserola**. The latter is over 1,640 feet high and enables you to trace the Catalan coastline and identify the streets and landmarks of Barcelona laid out below.

1. The modern shopping mall and nightspot Maremàgnum is located near the fish market and beaches where you can stretch out in the sun.

2. The Teleféric (cable car) across the port, opened in 1968, is an amusing way of getting a great view of the city. It runs 2,680 feet from the top of Montjuïc to the port. No view from land can match it.

3. At the end of the Rambla the monument to Columbus looks over the harbour. Built in 1886, it is an impressive iron column, crowned by a statue of the discoverer of America. Inspiring vistas over the port and the city. Take the elevator to the top for.

4. Before its four faces were installed in the 18th century, the clock tower was the port lighthouse. It is located at the point where Avinguda Paral.lel and Avinguda Meridiana would meet if they continued into the sea.

Green Barcelona

There is a good network of bicycle lanes in Barcelona. As time goes by, car and truck drivers are becoming more accustomed to the need to respect this form of transport. The broad, treelined strips of the wide avenues (Diagonal, Gran Via, Meridiana, etc) have been taken advantage of to encourage bicycling, which is a good way to visit the city's parks.

The **Parc de la Ciutadella** is the largest park near the downtown area. Another fascinating green area is **Parc Güell**, one of the remarkable creations of the architect Antoni Gaudí. His original aim was to design a residential area for the elite of Barcelona's society one hundred years ago. However, the project did not work. Instead, the city converted the space into a public park imbued with great serenity.

The **Parc de l'Espanya Industrial** is a fine example of what can be done when land is reclaimed from factory areas. The old building in the middle has been converted into a centre for social activities. Around the park lies the unpretentious neighbourhood of Sants.

There are many other pockets of green around the city: the **Parc del Laberint**, the gardens **Mossèn Costa i Llobera** with a fascinating botanical garden, the **Parc del Guinardó**, the gardens of **Palau de Pedralbes**, the **Turó del Putxet** and the **Parc de la Guineueta**.

However, the true lungs of the city are the **Parc de Collserola**, a natural reserve to the northwest separating the city from the towns on the other side of the Collserola mountain range. Here you can find all types of local flora and fauna. The **carretera de l'Arrabassada** and the **carretera de Vallvidrera** lead up into this refreshing countryside, where there is always the option of stopping off at a picnic ground in **Les Planes** or **La Floresta**.

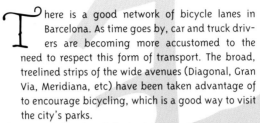

1. A bird's eye view of the Parc de la Ciutadella, the site of the Universal Exposition of 1888.

2. The Parc de la Trinitat was created during of the urban redesign of 1992. Located within one of the junctions of the new city beltway, there are seven hectares of rich vegetation, an amphitheatre and a sports area.

On the previous page

3. The waterfall in the Parc de la Ciutadella was designed by Josep Fontseré. The stairs lead to the arch, crowned by a wrought iron sculpture of the four-horse chariot of Aurora, the goddess of the dawn.
4. The Parc del Litoral is a good example of how the areas along the shore have been reincorporated back into the city.
5. The grounds on which the Palau de Pedralbes was built were donated by Eusebi Güell, Antoni Gaudí's sponsor.
6. Aware of the environment's importance, City Hall has multiplied by three the size of the green spaces. There are now far more parks than those created by the two expositions.

On this page

7. The Parc del Laberint is on the old site of the estate of the Marques of Llupià i Alfarràs. This magnificent neoclassic garden is on three levels, and its name comes from the maze dating from the 18th century.

8, 9, 10. Casually strolling around the many parks and gardens of Barcelona enables you to see in a great number of sculptures by different artists with diverse styles.

11. The Parc de Montjuïc is beautiful in its own right, but it also offers unbeatable views over the city and the port.

Barcelona neighbourhoods

arcelona is organised administratively into different municipalities. The current layout of the city is the fruit of the creeping expansion of Barcelona as it gradually absorbed the villages around it. This process began in 1859 according to the urban plan of the designer **Ildefons Cerdà**. This ambitious and deep-reaching project shaped what Barcelona has become today and spawned the **Eixample** grid system.

Cerdà's extraordinary idea was a grid of streets perpendicular and parallel to the sea that formed square blocks with green spaces in the middle. The street intersections form rhombuses rather than right-angled corners. Two diagonals cut through the streets and relieve the rigidity, while three roads connect the new urban area with the old. However, the plan was never fully implemented because of the pressure of property developers and the permissiveness of successive city councils.

The Cerdà Plan was put into effect from 1860 to 1868 and coincided with a surge in the populations of what are now districts within Barcelona: **Sant Gervasi**, **Les Corts**, **Hostafrancs**, **Poble Nou** and **Sant Martí de Provençals**. These districts were little villages just outside the area previously defined by the city walls. Sant Martí was popularly known as the "Manchester of Spain". All these changes to the urban landscape aided the incorporation of the outskirts into the city proper although the task was slow and arduous, and even sometimes traumatic.

Advances in transportation gradually made life more comfortable from 1884 onwards and ended the relative isolation of these suburbs. Nevertheless, it was not until 1897 that **Gràcia**, **Sants**, **Sant Andreu**, **Sant Gervasi** and **Sant Martí** formally formed part of the Catalan capital. The result was that by 1900 the population had increased to above half a million.

The economic strength of Barcelona during this period meant that the city was constantly being improved although it was still in the throes of change. **Horta**, **Sarrià** and **Vallvidrera** were yet to be incorporated - this happened between 1904 and 1921- and the link roads between these hamlets and the city centre were still in need of renovation. The old city also had to be reformed.

1. The Born market, which dates from 1876, was the site of the jousting tournaments in the Middle Ages. Today it is being restored to house the Provincial Library; its 13,950 square feet will convert it into the largest in the city.

The different areas of the city have slowly acquired their own personality, which is heavily influenced by the past. Fortunately, their character has not been totally wiped out by their incorporation into the metropolitan zone. It is easy to understand how ways of life and the atmosphere varies from neighbourhood to neighbourhood.

Ciutat Vella has all the characteristics of the traditionally old part of the city: a warren of streets dotted with historic buildings, art museums and antique and curiosity shops worth browsing. Ciutat Vella is next to Plaça Catalunya and the commercial area Portal de l'Angel. It has become fashionable to dine out in this area and there are many bars and restaurants were visitors can enjoy out good local food. On Friday and Saturday nights, and during the vacation periods, the area is quite lively.

It is impossible to think of the **Eixample** without realising the role played by the street grid structure. Eixample is the location of offices, the regional offices of the banks, the magnificent shops along Passeig de Gracìa and graceful Rambla Catalunya, art galleries and modernist architecture. Investment in property means that old apartment blocks are being replaced with modern buildings as soon as planning permission is granted.

Gràcia has become fashionable because it has managed to preserve its small village charm as well as offering a rich mix of bars, cafés, cinemas and theatres. The Plaça del Sol, in the middle of a maze of narrow streets, is a pedestrian zone full of life, especially from the afternoon through to the early morning hours. The neighbourhood is also brimming with little traditional shops, while the busy thoroughfare Gran de Gràcia accommodates more mainstream shopping facilities. This was the Roman road that linked Barcino with the Castro Octavio of Sant Cugat.

More local shopping is located along **Carretera de Sants**. This street has a high number of medium-sized shops demonstrating the strength of the family-run business in Catalonia. Sants forms part of the district of **Sants-Montjuïc** whose character was forged by the presence of the railway station, numerous factories (giving rise to some social

2. The Plaça del Sol is the most colourful square in Gràcia. This space, tranquil during the day, comes to life at night as people attracted by the lively atmosphere converge on it.

3. The Plaça Reial, constructed on the site of an old convent of Capuchin Friars, was conceived as an imitation of the royal French courtyards. The sculpture in the middle, *Les Tres Gràcies*, and the ten surrounding lampposts are the work of Antoni Gaudí.

4. The Pont del Treball was designed by the renowned architect Santiago Calatrava. As in most of his works, it combines cutting edge technology with organic forms.

5. The Mossèn Costa i Llobera park on the slopes of Montjuïc is the home of a wide variety of exotic and tropical plants, some of the cactus being as high as three metres. The park offers fine views over the port of Barcelona.

unrest), local amateur sports clubs, and a strong trade union presence. These elements, combined with the neighbourhood's population of 30,000, help explain Sants's flavor.

The district of **Les Corts** used to be fields dotted with grand farmhouses (masies). Today, in its area of 5.5 square kilometres, it is possible to identify ten different neighbourhoods. Within the district, the residences become more upscale moving away from the city centre. The area is dominated by the world famous **Camp Nou**, home of Barcelona Football Club, built in 1957 and designed by **Francesc Mitjans** with the collaboration of **Josep Soteras** and **Lorenzo García Barbón**.

The district of **Sarrià-Sant Gervasi** is located in the upper part of the city. It combines the quaint allure of the small village which Sarrià once was with the modern blocks of spacious flats which run from Passeig Sant Gervasi to Passeig Bonanova.

Nou Barris, which in Catalan means new neighbourhoods, is the result of the vertiginous population growth which Catalonia experienced in the Fifties and Sixties. Unfortunately, it was built too hastily and with a lack of forethought. However, in the Nineties wide avenues and broadwalks were constructed to make it a more comfortable place.

During the process of industrialisation, many factories and warehouses were built in **Sant Martí**. Workers traditionally lived near the companies in Clot, Sagrera and Poblenou. Now, some new middle class owners have moved in alongside the families that have been living there for two or three generations and the area has undergone serious renovation. Many factories and warehouses have been converted into New York style lofts, proving a hit with students, artists, architects and young couples without children. The city council is backing Poblenou as the home for new dot com companies. These new industries neither pollute nor make noise and are therefore ideal for the residents.

On the edge of Barcelona is the district of **Sant Andreu**, known as Sant Andreu del Palomar when it was formerly a separate town. One of the oldest parts of the city, is created a reputation for its determination to stand up for its rights during the strife after the

6. Some remains of the industrialisation, that took place at the end of the XIX century, can still be seen. These three chimneys were considered worth saving as part of the industrial heritage of the city, but the factory was knocked down.

7, 8. The speed with which Barcelona grew from the mid XIX century onwards can be appreciated in these two photos of Avinguda Diagonal. When Josep Puig i Cadafalch took on the assignment of constructing the Casa de les Punxes in 1903, this avenue still cut through open green spaces. It was soon to become a central thoroughfare of the developing city.

Industrial Revolution of 1871. Today, life in the district revolves around the Carrer Gran de Sant Andreu, the old Roman road that leads into Clot and towards the city centre.

Horta-Guinardó is the third largest district and includes the old village of Horta, the zone created for the Olympic games when the Vall d'Hebron was renovated, and the area around Vallcarca. Horta is by far the most traditional and historic neighbourhood since it was an independent municipality with its own character before it became part of Barcelona.

10. The *Capsa de Mistos*, by Cla Oldenburg (1992), symbolis of the Olympics. It represen the fire of the torch and the crouching matches represen the power of the triumphal athletes.

9. The Velòdrom, built where a dog track used to be, was the first Olympic installation to go up in the run up to the 1992 Games.

11. The Rambla, a highly
emblematic street in
Barcelona, presents the
multiple faces of the city.
The Rambla is included in
any tour of the city's
medieval sites.

12. The plurality of cultures
and people present in
Barcelona encourage
tolerance and life
without strife.

infrastructure

arcelona is a cosmopolitan and economically dynamic city which has placed faith in projects whose aim is to build a better future. The city planners have always been aware that to be modern and to ensure that the city is a competitive site for business investment and head offices, good infrastructures are essential.

Holding the Olympic Games in Barcelona was a great opportunity to modernise all aspects of the city, and the Cultural Forum of 2004 is sure the next occasion for city-wide improvements.

An important network of trains and highways links the Catalan capital with other Catalan provinces and with the rest of Spain and Europe. El Prat airport and the port guarantee connections to anywhere in the world by air or sea. And an effective public transportation system makes it easy to get around the city.

Large scale public works an enlargement of the airport, the arrival of the TGV and the installation of modern telecommunications systems will allow the city to face the future with confidence.

1. Barcelona's port is one of the busiest in the western Mediterranean. It connects the Ciutat Condal with the Balearic Islands, Italy and France.
2. Sea trade has always been a great boost to the city's economy. The volume of freight currently being shipped in both directions through the port is over 50 million tons.
3. The Porta d'Europa is the new bridge that rises up to let ships pass. It joins the city with the old breakwater in the Port Vell, next to the passenger terminal and the docks. It was opened in June 2000 and is 3,780 feet long. Each of the steel sheets that make it up weighs around 2,000 tons.

4. El Prat airport was modernized for the Olympic Games of 1992, enabling it to handle the more than 10 million passengers and 70,000 tons of freight that go through it every year. Its importance to Spain is reflected by the fact that 20 per cent of all domestic flights either take off or land in Barcelona. However, demand is so high that construction is now underway to double the passenger capacity and to multiply the freight handled by eight.

5. Barcelona is the centre of the European services of Renfe, the national railway company. The expres trains to Paris, Zurich, Geneva and Milan leave from França rail station.
6. Three motorways lead out of Barcelona. Two run along the coast towards the north (Girona) and the south (Tarragona). The other one heads towards Lleida.

The Barri Gòtic

The Gothic area lies at the heart of the city. Although popularly known as the **Barri Gòtic**, this name is not entirely accurate because there are other architectura styles besides Gothic.

The **cathedral of Barcelona** is at the centre of the Barri Gòtic. It was finished in the 15th century, and its choir, crypt and cloister are especially noteworthy. Four galleries lead to a lush garden and Gothic fountain. The roof-top terrace offers striking views of the city. The façade provides a splendid backdrop for the times when *sardanes* (a traditional Catalan dance with many people joining hands) are performed in the square before the cathedral, or for the Santa Llúcia fair just before Christmas at which you can buy Christmas trees or figures for Nativity scenes.

Another place which offers great views of the city is the **Mirador de Martí l'Huma**, a Renaissance tower distinguished by its seven floors of arched windows, five on each level. Right next to it stands the **Palau Reial Major** dating from the 13th century. Also worth visiting is the nearby **Acadèmia de Bones Lletres**, the largest private medieval palace, built on the Roman walls in the 13th century. Equally impressive are the **Pati Llimona**, the **Palau Centelles** and the **Palau Moixó**, which has a beautiful patio from the 18th century.

It is interesting to stroll through the old Jewish neighbourhood, the **Call**. The only trace remaining is a Hebrew stone plaque in Carrer Marlet. In 1391 more than one thousand Jews where shamefully murdered in an attack. Shortly afterwards, in 1401, Jews were expelled from the city.

Visitors always end up finding their way to the **church of Santa Maria del Pi**, a Gothic construction in a square where buskers and

1. The gentle trickle of water, a family of white geese and a small garden surrounded by high arches make the cloister one of the most relaxing corners of the cathedral.

4

2. Inspired by the Sighing Bridge in Venice, this neoclassic gallery crosses the Carrer del Bisbe and joins the Palau de la Generalitat with the Casa dels Canonges, the Medieval palace which is the official residence of the president of Catalonia.

3. The Palau Reial Major, residence of the Condes de Barcelona from the 9th century onwards, includes the Tinell room, where it is said that Columbus was presented to Catholic Kings when he returned from discovering America.
A piece by Eduardo Chillida sits alongside medieval decorations.

painters congregate to display their arts on Sundays mornings. Little food stalls are set up selling traditional local products like honey, cheese, cookies and sweet cakes. One of the streets leading out of the Plaça del Pi is the **Carrer Petritxol**, full of plaques commemorating events which took place on this narrow street. Its art galleries are famous and those with a sweet tooth can enjoy a cup of hot chocolate.

The most notable example of Gothic architecture is the **church Santa Maria del Mar**. Its two twin octagonal towers reach the sky and it is divided inside into three impressively stark naves.

So many cultural offerings, the unique character of the quarter and the fact that most squares are pedestrian-only make this an ideal area for exploring.

On this page

4. The Plaça del Rei is packed with architectural gems. As well as the Palau Reial Major, there is the Santa Àgata chapel, the lookout of the King Martí and the Palau del Lloctinent, which today contains the archive of the crown of Aragón.

5. Built on top of the Roman fortress at the end of the 15th century in Gothic style, the Casa de l'Ardiaca (Archdeacon's residence) today houses the city's historical archive. The Archdeacon represented the church's power over legal matters.

6. The prosperity generated by trade in Barcelona in the Middle Ages is reflected in the beauty of the architecture. As you stroll through the quarter you will constantly come across curious details like a lintel, a gargoyle, an arch or a patio.

7. On top of the Palau de la Generalitat sits the carillon, a set of 49 bells which chime for the festival de la Mercè.

8. The church of Santa Maria was built in a relatively short period of time, 55 years, which meant that its style is very defined. It is the most representative piece of Gothic Catalan architecture. Spacious naves, excellent acoustics and stained glass windows from the 15th and 18th centuries all add up to make it well worth visiting. Unfortunately, the choir was destroyed by fire during the Civil War (1936-1939).

1. Cathedral of Barcelona
2. Mirador de Martí l'Humà and Palau Reial Major
3. Acadèmia de Bones Lletres
4. Pati Llimona
5. Palau Centelles
6. Palau Moixó
7. Call
8. Church Santa Maria del Pi
9. Church Santa Maria del Mar
10. Palau de la Generalitat
11. Casa dels Canonges
12. Casa de l'Ardiaca

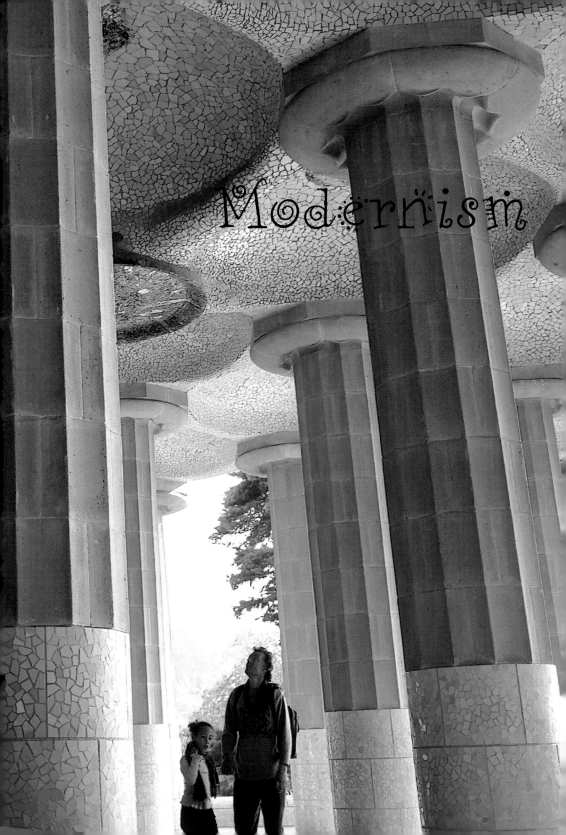

Modernism

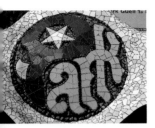

*A*t the end of the 19th century Barcelona was booming. Money was coming in from exports as the most successful businessmen amassed fortunes. In turn, credit houses were on the lookout for clients, and lifestyles changed under the influence of this new wealth distribution.

The newly emerged social class of factory owners and brokers was much more ostentatious than the rather staid nobility. Entrepreneurs quickly set up scores of restaurants where, alongside the theatre, the new elite could see and be seen.

It was in this context that Catalan **Modernism** was born, an artistic movement known in other European countries as Art Nouveau or Modern Style. In Barcelona it was linked to support for the Catalan culture and language and developed by invigorating architects such as **Antoni Gaudí**, **Domènech i Montaner**, **Puig i Cadalfach** and others, less known but of equal importance, like **Sagnier** and **Granell**. The vitality of their works is unique and their designs are some of the most delightful aspects of the city.

The new industrial bourgeoisie and bankers made architecture the key for declaring social status. They commissioned grand houses and a favourite spot was along Passeig de Gràcia. Today, in general, these apartment buildings, like **Casa Milà**, **Casa Amatller** and **Casa Batlló**, conserve the name of the original owners, who were more interested in elegance than thriftiness. However, Modernism also filtered down to more modest façades, and pharmacies, cake shops, bakeries and other high street establishments brightened up the city, offsetting the pragmatism of industrialisation. The **Modernist route** is well marked out in guidebooks, or in free pamphlets for tourists. The route includes 50 buildings, most located in the Eixample and Ciutat Vella.

1. The dragon of Parc Güell is one of the most emblematic sculptures of Catalan Modernism.
2. Gaudí let his imagination ran wild when designing the square in Parc Güell. The curves and the Jujol mosaics will leave the visitor wondering what the rest of his creations are like.

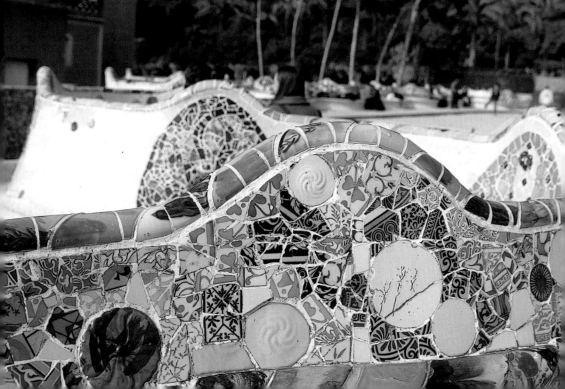

On this page

3. A close up of the hypostyle room, designed to house a market that supplied all the homes on the site.

4, 5. Gaudí conceived Parc Güell so that the magnificent architecture blended into the landscape of the beautiful garden.

6. The whole project, which included a city park and houses, was meant to recall English homes set on their own grounds.

On the next page

7, 8. All of Gaudí's genius is distilled in la Sagrada Família, his most ambitious project to which he dedicated 43 years. It is planned that 12 spires representing the disciples will be completed.

On the next page

14. Gaudí's idea behind la Pedrera was to design a giant sculptured building, a seascape of underwater caves coming together to exalt the virtues of curved lines.
15. The roof is dotted with Venetian style sculptured chimneys.
16. The vestibule, once the coach house, leads down into what was an underground garage, now converted into an auditorium.
17. The Casa Batlló is one of the most beautiful buildings in Barcelona. There are three interesting elements on the façade: the multi-coloured tiles, the highly decorative wrought iron balcony railings and the undulating roof depicting Sant Jordi slaying the dragon.

On this page

9. The vault covering in the central nave of the expiatory temple is the most recently finished part of the Sagrada Família project.
10. The Passion façade was completed by Josep Maria Subirachs in the 1980s. His sculptures provide a point of contrast against the prevailing right-angled structures.
11. A close-up of an inscription on one of the spires. The style of the lettering is typically modernist.
12. The main façade of the Hospital de la Santa Creu i Sant Pau, relocated away from its old site in carrer Hospital, faces down Avinguda Gaudí towards la Sagrada Família, breaking the block rigidity of Eixample.
13. The architect Lluís Domènech i Montaner conceived a hospital made up of 48 pavilions laid out in a garden like a town, separated by streets 99 feet wide and two 164 feet avenues forming the axes. Underground tunnels connect the wards and different departments.

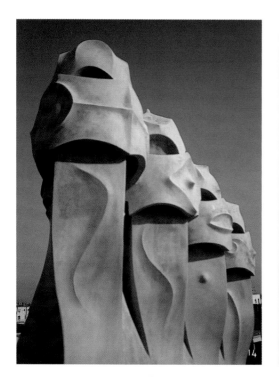

noves
abstrac-
cions

BIANCHI.BLECKNER.BROTO
DAVENPORT.DORNER.DUNHAM.ELLIS.
FÖRG.FRIZE.GARCÍA SEVILLA.
GORDILLO.GRAU.HALLEY.HEILMANN.
JENSSEN.KIRKEBY.LASKER.MERKEL.
McKEEVER.PRADAS.RAE.REED.
RICHTER.SCULLY.STEIR.TAAFFE.URZAY.
USLÉ.WINTERS.

Contemporary art

*A*n outward-looking city, Barcelona it has always attracted artists, and art is easily accessible at all levels. The first way of finding out what is happening on the Barcelona art scene is to visit the small or medium-sized art galleries, basically grouped into two areas. The first zone is along **Carrer Petritxol**, next to **Plaça del Pi**. The art galleries here are traditional family businesses. The other area where art galleries are concentrated is more upmarket. There are twelve showrooms on **Carrer Consell de Cent**, on the two blocks between **Passeig de Gràcia** and **Carrer Balmes**.

If you want to visit works that have passed the test of time there is a good selection of museums to choose from. The **Museu d'Art Modern** located in the Parc de la Ciutadella houses paintings, sculptures and decorative arts.

The **Museu Picasso** cannot be missed. It is a challenging collection which includes drawings and paintings from Picasso's formative years. His interpretations of Velázquez's *Las Meninas* deserve special mention. Other worthwhile visits include the **Fundació Antoni Tàpies**, which exhibits a complete collection by this emblematic present day Catalan artist, including the sculpture crowning the building. And finally, to stimulate the mind as well as the eye, head up Montjuïc to the **Fundació Joan Miró** where a permanent collection is on show as well as rotating exhibitions lent out by other museums around the world.

Lovers of cutting edge art should visit the **Museu d'Art Contemporani de Barcelona** (MACBA). Not only does it shed light on 20th century styles, but it also simbolises the determination to renovate the Raval neighbourhood. The **Centre de Cultura Contemporània de Barcelona** (CCCB), dedicated to urban art and modern artistic expressions, is also worth seeing.

1. The MACBA, designed by the prestigious architect Richard Meier, was made possible thanks to the important economic contribution of the Catalan government and generous private donations. Together with the CCCB, it has enabled the regeneration of the Raval quarter.

MUSEU D'ART CONTEMPORANI DE

2. Fernando Botero, sticking to his "fat is beautiful" motif, created this sculptured located next to Drassanes.
3. Josep Lluís Sert designed the Fundació Joan Miró on a site with splendid views over the city, accentuated by the many slopes of the concrete volume.

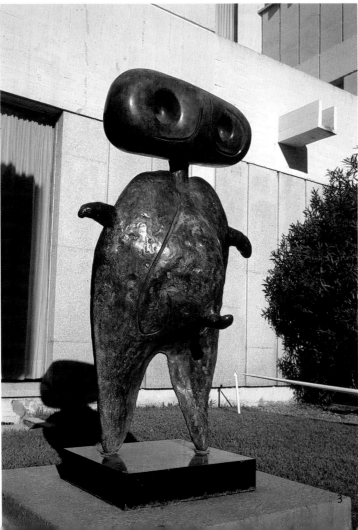

4. The Fundació Antoni Tàpies, a genuine homage to contemporary art, is located in a modernist building designed in 1882 by Domènech i Montaner. The building was originally built as the headquarters of the publishing company Montaner i Simon. The cable work of art on the roof, *La cadira i el núvol* (The Chair and the Cloud) is controversial, and has as many fans as detractors.

Many walls around the city are covered in *graffiti*. Originally appearing in the Eighties in New York, *graffiti* art work is normally associated with alternative lifestyles and displays a rejection of established values. However, some artists see it as a legitimate way of getting their art onto the streets.

Barcelona living

Multicultural
Barcelona

arcelona is an open city that strives to make visitors and new residents feel at home. A stroll down the street demonstrates that Barcelona is a melting pot and that people from all over the world must live together in harmony. The city's ethnic diversity is perhaps most visible on the emblematic walkway, the Rambla.

The Rambla, from Plaça Catalunya downwards, is amazingly colourful and a great location for observing the human race. Human statues and other street performers line the walkway. As the Catalan singer Joan Manuel Serrat said everybody can act however they like. There's no need to turn their back on their roots, only to accept everybody else the way they are.

1. Urban tribes provide a radical, colourful touch to the city.

2. The gardens and parks are full of people practicing petanque, a traditional Catalan sport. The winner is the player who manages to get one of their throws the nearest to the jack.

3. In the centre of the city there are still shoe shiners who, for a modest sum, will get your shoes to glisten with a good dose of polish and a rub.

4. The live statues of Barcelona are justifiably building up a reputation. Dressed up as historical or fictitious characters, they are capable of standing still out for four hours without so much as blinking, although they may make a slight movement if you drop a coin into their hat. The statues have acquired such a name for themselves that they have formed a guild and started to organize tours round Europe.

Traditions

Barcelona has cultivated traditions and customs celebrated year after year. The city's calendar of fiestas is full and varied. As well as the traditional celebrations shared with all of Spain (Christmas, Easter and Carnival), there are many other dates on which the people of Catalonia organise what could be defined as street parties. Each town has its own individual "city fiesta", normally corresponding to its Patron Saint.

The 17th of January is the **Cavalgada dels Tres Tombs** in honour of Sant Antoni, the Patron Saint of Animals. On this day, the people bless their pets.

February is when the happiness and fun of **Carnival** spills out onto the streets as the children dress up and put on masks. The Barcelona to Sitges old car rally is also held in February.

On March 3rd the neighbours of Gràcia celebrate **Sant Medir**. The *colles* (groups of neighbours) ride in a horse and cart and throw sweets to the onlookers and delighted children.

On April 23rd is the celebration of **Sant Jordi**, the day of the book and the rose. Barcelona is awash with the colour of roses as stalls of flowers and books are set up all over the city, and across Catalonia.

In May the **Jocs Florals** fiesta is celebrated. May 11th is the fiesta of **Sant Ponç**, when Carrer Hospital is decked out with stalls selling aromatic and medicinal plants, jams and syrups in honour of the Patron Saint of herbalists.

Corpus Christi has been celebrated in Barcelona since the beginning of the 14th century. Parades of giants and figures with large heads called *cabezudos* file through the streets, and in the cloister of the cathedral visitors contemplate the conservation of a curious tradition, *l'ou com balla*. An egg is literally made to dance, cradled by the water spouting out of the fountain decked in flowers for the occasion.

The summer solstice is one of the most important party nights in Catalonia. **Sant Joan** on the 23rd of June celebrates shortest night of the year. The Catalans celebrate the date by dining in the open air and setting off fireworks into the night sky. This is not an event for those with sensitive ears. The other *verbenas* in the Ciutat Condal are Sant Pere (June 29th) and Sant Jaume (July 25th).

1. In every *sardana* ring there is a dancer who must mark time and indicate the change of step.

2. The *flabiol* is the instrument used to play the principal tune of the *cobla*.

3. The *timbaler* (drummer) is a very significant person in the popular festivals. One legend has it that during the Napoleonic war a little drummer boy was capable of frightening the French army away. When they heard his beating drum, magnified by the Bruc mountains, they thought a great battalion was coming towards them.

4. Often these *gegants* represent characters from Catalan rural life, like the heir to the family estate or the head of the family.

Throughout summer, the **Grec** cultural program, one of the most important in Europe, is held. Plays, dances, concerts and other cultural activities are performed under the nearly cloudless Mediterranean sky.

During the hottest month, August, many districts of Barcelona celebrate their *festa major*. The most popular are that of Gràcia, which comes first on the calendar, and that of Sants on the other side of the city one week later. The neighbours form groups and convert their streets into fantastic settings, a moonscape, the far west or an enchanted forest. A popular jury decides which street wins for the best decoration. The dancing, for all the family, continues well into the night. Local residents do not get much sleep during the *festa major*.

The ɪɪth of September is the national day of Catalonia, the **Diada**, and then thir-

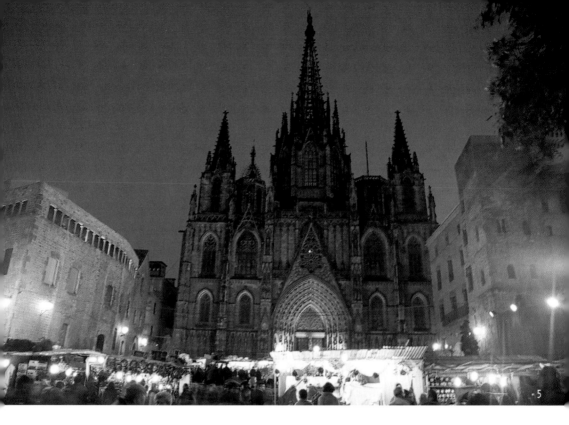

5. The Santa Llúcia fair, dating back over 200 years, never fails to bring a smile to the children's faces. In the stalls set up around the cathedral just before Christmas, everything is available for building a Nativity scene at home.

teen days later, on the 24th, begins the **Festa de la Mercè**, the Patron Saint of Barcelona. Fantastic creatures, *correfocs*, parade through the streets spitting fire and fireworks light up the sky. Old and young dance *sardanes* (a Catalan dance) and children participate in sports days and a whole host of other activities. On September 29th Barceloneta celebrates its *festa major*, **Sant Miquel**.

In the first days of December, the square in front of the cathedral is packed with Christmas trees and candles for sale for the fair of **Santa Llúcia**.

During many of these festivals it is possible to observe Catalan traditions such as *sardanes*, *castells* (human towers), *correfocs* and *gegants*.

The *sardana* is the most popular typical Catalan dance. Its origins go back as far as the old dance known as the *contrapàs* and the *sardana* is danced to the rhythm of *cobles* (little orchestras). Though the dance is precise and it is useful to count if you want to stay in line with the other dancers, it is not difficult to get the hang of it.

The *castells* (human towers) appear to touch the sky and represent, like no other spectacle, the importance of working as a team. The stoutest people form the bottom layer of the tower, and other team members climb up their shoulders until a pinnacle is formed at the top. This is a risky, but ancient Catalan tradition, and watching the tower rise is breathtaking.

Fire is a vital part of Catalan folklore. Bonfires play an important role on Sant Joan and in the **correfocs**, when devils run through the street spreading hell's flames as they playfully chase the public with torches, sprinklers and crackers.

Gegants (giants) are a leftover from the ancient celebrations of the Corpus. Dancers are disguised as a legend or a famous character out of Catalan history by wearing masks and figures made out of papier-maché.

6. Part of the fun of the Barcelona to Sitges car rally is to observe the classic cars and the driver's period costumes.

7

7. Sant Jordi is the day of the book and the rose. According to tradition men give a rose to women, who in turn give them a book. However, many women are beginning to receive both a rose and a book.

8. On the 25th December a group of swimmers cross Barcelona's port. This tradition, started by a headlong dive into the very cold waters, goes back to the Twenties.

9. The most daring participants of the *correfocs* mix foolhardiness with courage running next to the devils spitting out fire. A word of advice for anyone who wants to participate: wear cotton clothes and cover your head and mouth.

9

Barcelona offers a wealth of activities for a great day on the town. Though some sights should be not be missed, there is something for everyone. On the top of Mount **Tibidabo** there is an attraction park where you can ride on the Helter Skelter or go through the ghost tunnel. The **Aquàrium** of Barcelona, located in Maremàgnum, houses a vast collection of marine life from penguins through to sharks and vividly coloured fish. The **Poble Espanyol** is a typical Spanish model town which can be visited like a museum. Or you can walk around Eixample admiring the Modernist buildings or walk down the Rambla to the port. Barcelona offers options galore and a vitality that few cities can match.

1. The Golondrina boat service came into operation in 1888 and has been taking tourists across the port from Portal de la Pau to the breakwater ever since.
2. Installed very near to the zoo and the França rail station, this hot air balloon tethered to the ground rises up to 150 metres to offer spectacular views across the city. Together with the balloon in the André Citroën park in Paris, it is the highest tethered balloon in the world.
3. Inaugurated in 1901, the Tramvia Blau is one of the most charismatic means of transport in the city. It is a pleasant way of going up the Mount Tibidabo.

4. The 64 cabins of the Telefèric (cable car) can be accessed from three points: one in the towers of the port, and the other two along Moll de la Fusta.
5. Going around the city on an open decked bus called Bus Turístic is a great way to see the sights. Passengers can get off and back on as many times as they like around the route.

8

On the previous page

6. Constructed for the Olympic Games of 1992, the Collserola telecom tower designed by Norman Foster has 13 floors. On the tenth there is a 560-metre high observation deck from which one can enjoy magnificent views over the city.

7. The shopping mall and leisure centre Maremàgnum contains a multi-cinema, an Imax cinema with a giant screen, a wide range of shops, restaurants, discos, bars and one of the biggest aquariums in the world.

On this page

8, 9, 10. There is a wide range of theatre on offer in Barcelona, going from fringe through to mainstream and classic plays, as well as dance, ballet and musicals. The classically inspired Teatre Nacional (9), designed by the architect Ricard Bofill has a floor space of 18,600 square feet covered by a metal roof held up by 26 columns that are 40 feet. Behind its glass front, many plays have been staged on since it was opened in 1996. Another grand project designed to enhance the city's cultural scene is the Auditori (10). This concert hall includes a symphonic sala and a multi-use hall. In the future it will house a museum dedicated to music and the Escola Superior de Música de Catalunya.

9

10

11. Barcelona is home to Europe's biggest aquarium. In its tanks there are over 300 species of marine life, some of them very rare, exotic or spectacular, such as the sharks. There is a specialized scientific library, video displays, a conference room, souvenir shop and restaurant.

12. The Castell dels Tres Dracs in the Parc de la Ciutadella houses the Museu de Zoologia. There is a permanent exposition as well as temporary exhibitions that allow the visitor explore the animal world. There is also a bookshop and library.

13, 14. The Barcelona zoo is one of the best in Europe in terms of the number of animals and their living conditions. The star of the show, "Floquet de neu" ("Snowflake"), the world's only albino gorilla in captivity, is an icon for the city. Within the zoological grounds, there are shows, children's attractions, a restaurant and a souvenir shop.

15, 16, 17. Tibidabo, also known as the Magic Mountain, is Barcelona's only attractions park. It was established in 1899. All that remains of that epoch is the Museu dels Autòmates, the renovated Aeromàgic, designed in 1935, and the aeroplane that dates from 1928. However, the park is not just a collection of relics; there are numerous thrills to be had on the modern rides.

18. At the end of the Rambla lies the Reials Drassanes de Barcelona, from 1378, a singular example of civil architecture. Originally used for building ships, it now houses the Museu Marítim.

19. Visitors to the Museu de la Ciència are welcomed by a spectacular Foucault pendulum, a practical demonstration of the Earth's rotation. The museum is educational as well as stimulating. Numerous temporary expositions take place and there are rooms dedicated to optics, mechanics and perception, as well as a planetarium. The museum is housed in a building designed by the architect Domènech i Estapà at the beginning of the 20th century.

20. Over 300 famous people are represented in the Museu de Cera, and visit to the museum it is a relaxing way of finding out about the history of humanity.

21. The Monumental is the only bullring in the city still in business. A few years ago there were two, but Las Arenas, near Plaça Espanya, closed down. Apart from bullfights -the season starts in spring- concerts and circuses are also held in the ring and there is a museum.

18

19

20

21

26

On the previous page

22, 23, 24, 25. Formed between the 15th and 17th centuries, the Rambla
has a different name along each of its five stretches. Kiosks, flower
stalls, pet shops, artists and passers by share this street stage.

On this page

26. A symbol of the Barcelona bourgeoisie, el Gran Teatre del Liceu was
inaugurated in 1848. Two fires, in 1861 and 1994, and a bomb explosion
have marked its history. Since its reopening in October 1999, the
institution has enjoyed renewed success.

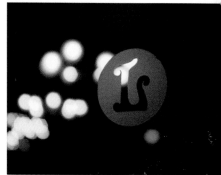

27, 28, 29. One of the best ways of experiencing Barcelona is to simply wander through its streets, parks and squares, mingling with the people. Inevitably you will come across hidden retreats where you can relax and enjoy works of art. *La Dona del Paraigües* (Lady with an Umbrella) (29) is in the Parc de la Ciutadella and *La Dona i l'ocell* (The Woman and the Bird) (27) is in the Parc de l'Escorxador. The Palau de Pedralbes also offers fine artwork (27).

27

28

29

30. Founded by Elisenda de Montcada in 1326, the Gothic cloister of Pedralbes monastery is one of the most spacious in the world. Today, it houses part of the Thyssen-Bornemisza collection of art.

31. It is impossible to come to Barcelona without strolling around Plaça Catalunya, the centre of the city and the departure point for many tours. On one side there is a monument to Francesc Macià, the first elected president of the Generalitat de Catalunya.

32, 33. Built between 1926 and 1929 with the intention of bringing together samples of the most representative Spanish architecture, on the same site Poble Espanyol has become a theme area where it is possible to walk leisurely, buy handicraft products, enjoy concerts, have dinner or dance at one of the discos.

32

33

34, 35, 36. Visiting the stadium of FC Barcelona is obligatory for sports fans, and especially, for the football enthusiasts. Camp Nou, inaugurated in 1957, has been the setting for some of the team's most spectacular moments. The stadium, the largest in Europe and the second largest in the world, is home to a museum that depicts the history of FC Barcelona. The impressive complex also includes a souvenir shop, a mini-stadium and a restaurant.

36

Gastronomy

1, 2, 3. The first vineyards were introduced on the Iberian Peninsula through the Catalan coast in the 5th century B.C., probably by the ancient Carthaginians. The Romans exploited their knowledge to produce wine, but it was not until between the 10th and the 14th centuries, that Catalonia's vines began to flourish as a business.

Barcelona's style and elegance has filtered down to its restaurants; or maybe it is the other way around and Barcelona's rich diversity and high quality of life begins with its balanced, healthy, varied and authentic diet. The dishes are based on natural, seasonal products that can be bought in any of the 40 markets spread around the city. These markets in themselves are worth a visit because they are genuine exhibitions of food: the stalls of meat, fish, fruit and vegetables are colourful displays. The most popular and also the most famous for the quality of its product range is the **Boqueria** (1840) located at the heart of the Ramblas. Its impressive wrought iron structure is reminiscent of other European markets of the same period. The **Sant Antoni market** is worth a visit on Sunday morning when second hand books, magazines, comics and CDs are exchanged.

If you are looking to check out different types of cooking, Barcelona is a wise destination. Chefs from all over Catalonia and Spain come here to ply their trade. As well as Catalan cooking, Spain boasts four other great regional cuisines: those of Galicia, Castile, the Basque country, and Andalucia. All of them are served in the restaurants of Barcelona alongside *nouvelle cuisine*, fast food and exotic oriental dishes.

It is impossible to draw up a complete list, even more so considering the turnover in new eateries, but we will highlight some of the places worth trying.

On the waterfront, great seafood is served at **Agua**. **La Provença** restaurant is outstanding: its dishes are hearty and it is popular among locals. Warm dishes are served in the minimalist interior of **Pou Dolç**. For couples who want an intimate meal with soft French music in the background, an ideal choice is **El Bristot de Bruno**. If you want to combine theatre with a well-served meal, the **Teatre Nacional de Catalunya** fits the bill. **La Flauta** offers quick food based on thin baguettes with appetising fillers. Basque restaurants are thriving: try the tapas at **Euskal Etxea**. Traditional Catalan food is the order of the day at **Senyor Parellada** in an atmosphere which conserves the original *fonda* (inn) feel. **La Vaqueria** has also remained faithful to the original architectural design and is the place to go if you are in the mood for meat and potatoes. The owner of

4. Today Catalonia is the region of Spain which produces the greatest number of registered wines, many of them worthy of international recognition. The wines from the county of Priorat are especially recommended. Catalonia also produces many cavas, its own dry sparkling wine.

Semproniana believes that the success of a restaurant depends on the helpfulness of the managers: you will be well looked after here. In **Quimet & Quimet** the standing tables are nearly always full and there is a pleasant village feel in the air. And if you want to feel that you have spent your evenings reading literature, drop into the splendidly decorated **Café Salambó** in Gràcia. **La Torreta de Gràcia** offers generous servings of traditional Catalan food. The **Rabasseda**, hidden away in the porches of an old convent, serves satisfying food and some quite elaborate dishes.

Maybe such a wide range of selections will bewilder you, but you can always consult the more detailed restaurant guidebooks to find out more about the Barcelona eating scene.

Another good deal in Barcelona is the traditional fixed price midday menu, which is usually hung just outside the restaurant. This menu allows you to sample homemade cuisine at a reasonable price.

The new formula of **Fres Co** is catching on. For a fixed price, you can help yourself to all you want from the dishes displayed on a counter in the middle of the restaurant. The menu includes pasta, vegetables, meats and other healthy foods.

Summing up, Barcelona is wonderfully alive with restaurants where eating is taken seriously.

5. Pouring wine down your throat from the long spout of a *porrón* is a traditional way of quenching your thirst as well as showing off your skill and dexterity.

5

6. Cava ferments in two stages. During the first stage, the grape juice is placed in stainless steel barrels for ten days. The second stage takes place in the wine cellars, which must maintain at a temperature of 14° to 16° centigrade for at least nine months. After this stage, during which the wine matures, the bottles are turned 180 degrees every day so that the sediments accumulate near the bottleneck and can be eliminated more easily. The wine is then ready for the final bottling and labelling.

7

7. The *tapeo* (eating small amounts of prepared dishes) is a habit acquired by the locals over recent years. Imported from other parts of the peninsula, it is now normal to find Catalans of all ages and social classes standing or sitting at the bars enjoying a wide variety of gastronomic delights. The quality is good and the service is fast.

8. The *esqueixada* is a traditional combination of cod, onion and tomato. In the past the fish arrived at the port in great quantities and could be conserved in salt: it was abundant and accessible. Now, it is mainly imported from Finland, and its price has gone up but it is still part of the diet of the people of Barcelona.
9. Grilled vegetables have an enriched flavour. Wild asparagus, courgettes, tomatoes, onions — in fact any vegetable — can be grilled and then seasoned with olive oil for a delicious taste.

10. Catalan cuisine has other ways of cooking vegetables, as shown by the *escalivada*. Peppers, aubergines and onions are placed in the oven and then afterwards covered up so that they continue to stew in their own juice.
11. Seafood is an important part of everybody's diet in Barcelona. Prawns, clams and mussels are easy to find in the markets, though not always at the price one would wish.

12, 13, 14. The cosmopolitan open-mindedness of the natives means that exotic restaurants abound. Keen to try out new gastronomic experiences from Japan, India, Pakistan, Lebanon, or any other corner of the world, the people of Barcelona frequent ethnic eateries.

15. No daily routine can skip coffee time. Whether it is served before the meal, or after it, in the morning or afternoon, the locals always find a moment to enjoy this drink that arrived from America over 400 years ago.

14

15

Shopping

Barcelona is a great city for people who love shopping. If you start off from the university zone of Avinguda Diagonal and work your way down past l'Illa shopping mall to Rambla Catalunya and Passeig de Gràcia, you will take in most of the famous flagship names in world fashion. The famous department store, El Corte Inglés, has three branches in Barcelona, and all of them are located along this route, as well as other Spanish establishments worth checking out, such as Zara, Mango, Massimo Dutti.

The shops which offer fashion at affordable prices are found along Portal de l'Àngel, Carrer Pelai and Carrer Portaferrisa. There are many shoe shops and plenty of establishments catering to young people and children. The recently opened shopping mall El Triàngle is in Plaça Catalunya, opposite El Corte Inglés, which has just opened a shop in the nearby Portal de l'Àngel dedicated exclusively to leisure including music, books and sports equipment.

If you want to delve into Barcelona's mercantile past it is best just to head off into the narrow maze of streets that make up Ciutat Vella and El Born. Many street names proclaim the activity that once went on there. For example, Carrer Argenteria was where the silversmiths did their trade. The antique shops on Carrer Canvis Vells, Carrer Princesa, Carrer del Rec and on Carrer Correus Vells are bursting with curious objects. In Carrer Rauric there is a delightful shop called **El Ingenio** selling disguises and fantastic masks known as *cabezudos*. In Carrer Vidreria there still stands a 100 year old business dedicated to the retailing of all sorts of crystal objects. Carrer Tallers has become the centre of record shops, and if you are looking for some obscure album, you will most likely be able to find it here.

Not long ago, City Hall decided to award a prize to the oldest, most popular and most original shops in the city, now identified with commemorative plaques. Among the winners one can find the wax and candle shop **Subirà** (1847) at number 7 Baixada de la Llibreteria; the chocolate shop **Farga**, dating from the beginning of the 19th century (on the corner of Carrer del Pi and Carrer Cucurulla), and the store **El Indio** (1830) in Carrer Carme.

1, 2, 3. Thanks to the good taste of the owners over the generations who wisely conserved the traditional shop front, today buying an aspirin, picking up a book by Cervantes or simply buying a cake can feel like taking a step back in time.

4. Some shop windows are worthy of attention in their own right. The cleverly combined and all-inclusive display of goods gives away the shopkeepers' profound knowledge of their trade.

5. Some shops selling the most modern product designs are in majestic buildings. The contrast between the façade and the window display is marked.

4

5

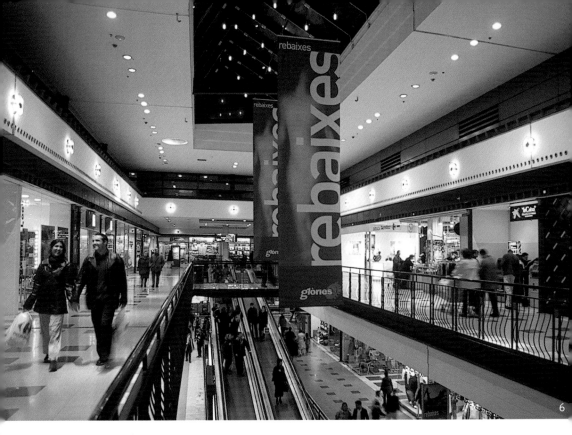

6

6. Shopping centres, increasingly common in Barcelona, offer the advantage of combining under one roof an extensive range of goods, underground parking, bank services, restaurants, cafés and cinemas.

7. In the old part of the city, a great number of boutiques have sprung up selling esoteric collections of wares: decorative objects imported from Africa, trendy clothes, natural fibre rugs, and paper lampshades. Endless, unexpected ideas that encourage you to rummage around in these establishments.

8. Lotteries are legal all across the Spanish state and a great many people try their luck in the Christmas lottery. On the day of the draw, a few days before Christmas Day, locals from all social classes tune into the radio as children chant out the fortunate numbers which decide the destination of the biggest prize, el Gordo (the fat one).

9. La Herboristeria del Rei was awarded the title of "supplier to the Royal Family" by Isabel II around 1857. Still true to its origins, this store sells over 220 medicinal herbs and spices.

10. Second hand articles are the order of the day at Els Encants market. Numerous curiosities, antique furniture, clothes, vinyl LPs, and other things thrown out by people emptying their homes in preparation for a move, are piled up in this open-air market by Les Glòries.

Barcelona at night

nother attraction for the tourists who come to Barcelona is the nightlife. Bars, live music, pubs, discos, concert halls and after-hours activity mean that nobody need go home early. Things are happening every day of the week but Thursday, Friday and Saturday are the busiest nights.

The best alternative and fringe scene is in the Ciutat Vella, especially around Plaça Reial, la Rambla and the maze of streets nearby. One sound option is to start in the bar **Glaciar**, move along to **Jamboree** for a bit of live music and end up in **La Macarena** dancing to Flamenco music. Alternatively, you may prefer to be your own guide, just wandering through the streets entering the bars that take your fancy as you come across them. If you head away from the Ramblas vaguely eastwards you will come to El Born, wich offers a variety of cocktail bars, like Miramelindo and Abaixadors Deu, as well as Basque-style tapas bars.

At the end of the Rambla you can cross the port to get to **Maremàgnum**, or turn left for the **Port Olímpic**. These two macro zones for having fun at night were created when Barcelona regained its shoreline at the time of the Olympic Games of 1992. Nowadays, they are true melting pots of people enjoying them-selves at night. There is a selection of every style and type of music from salsa through to funk or pop. Drinkers and socialisers with a sense of humour can try out **Baja Beach Club** where the waiters and wait-resses serve drinks in a bikini or swimming trunks.

In the Eixample, there are also many locals haunts, espe-cially in the Carrer Balmes and the Carrer Aribau. The **Nick Havana** bar has always been a favourite for its sleek decoration. Young singer-songwriters perform live in **Mediterráneo** and **Velvet**. These bars were originally frequented by the gay community but the easygoing atmosphere soon attracted all types of

1, 2, 3. Many modernist establishments were converted into bars and cafés during the late Nineties. Wrought iron columns, stained glass windows and the lovingly restored century-old furniture provide a proper setting for a good coffee, tapas or a meal.

people. Pamphlets explaining the gay scene in Barcelona are available.

Home to many artists and actors, Gràcia is also bursting with life when the sun goes down. In the Plaça del Sol there are many bars and cafés where you can take a drink. Start at the **Café del Sol** or **Sol Soler** and then wander off into the adjacent streets, full of bars where you can begin or end the night.

The upper part of Barcelona also offers imaginative places for meeting your friends, making new ones or dancing. **Mirablau**, perched over Barcelona at the top of Avinguda Tibidabo, has a

good atmosphere and splendid vistas over the city. A little further down Avinguda Tibidabo lies **Rosebud** with its pleasant garden, ideal for the sticky summer nights. Moving towards Diagonal, the block formed by the streets Amigó and Santaló is packed with bars buzzing at the weekend. One of the best known is **Universal**.

When the factory and warehouse area Poblenou began its transformation, not everything was turned into lofts or residences. There are many discos and bars, that are popular with the under twenty crowd. **Razzmatazz** is the most emblematic: it recently opened its doors on the site of what was a classic of Barcelona's nightlife and club scene, the gig venue Zeleste. **Bóveda**, **Be Good** and **L'Ovella Negra** complete the selection.

3, 4. The Casino de Barcelona was recently relocated. It had in fact been near Sitges, housed in a Versailles-style mansion, but is now in the Port Olímpic, much easier to get to, plus there is more space.

5. Some bars enjoy a location along the seashore. The clients can enjoy the dramatic views over the Mediterranean.

6. *Rumbas*, *sevillanas* and *charanga* music can be danced and heard in La Paloma dancing hall. All ages come here for entertainment.

7, 8. Salsa music encourages you to be daring, and although this type of music is found all across Barcelona, the cheekiest nightclubs are in the Port Olímpic.

9. Groups of friends tend to meet in a quiet café or bar at around 11 p.m. At roughly 1 a.m. the streets of Barcelona are full of young people moving on to the discos.

Barcelona's surroundings

One of Barcelona's strong points is its location, which enables visitors to enjoy many activities only a short drive out of the city. The Mediterranean's mild climate is ideal for outdoors activities, and two nearby industrial cities, **Terrassa** and **Sabadell**, offer cultural events. In the **Pyrenees**, the counties of **Cerdanya** and **Ripollès** offer numerous well-equipped ski resorts for tourists. There are hotels, mountain lodges, apartments for rent and companies providing adventure sports on the rivers. In spring, summer and fall many people from Barcelona head north to enjoy rural tourism.

There are beaches galore in Catalonia, some of them less than an hour's drive from Barcelona. To the north lies the **Costa Brava** (Wild Coast) with pine trees that lead down to rocks dropping into the sea. This stunningly beautiful part of the coast is dotted with little coves that are tucked away. **Sitges**, to the south, is renowned for the quality of its nightlife, the charm of the town centre and its tranquil sandy beaches.

As well as sunbathing and swimming, there are also some interesting museums to visit.

Other beautiful beaches can be found towards the south, on the **Costa Daurada** (Gold Coast) in Tarragona. Here, the water is warm, the beaches are wide and the sea is calm. Tarragona is also famous for its well-preserved Roman ruins, which reflect the splendour of this era.

The monastery of Montserrat, set high up in the mountains, is a spiritual home of the religious. The rocky outcrop is an imposing backdrop for the monastery.

1. The Museu Nacional de la Ciència i la Tècnica, is located in the Vapor Aymerich, a building dating from 1909, whose central nave has a floor space of over 9,300 square feet covered by vaults supported on wrought iron columns. The coal cellars and the 43 metre high chimney are worth visiting.

2. The 20,460 square feet of Parc de Sant Jordi (Terrassa) occupy part of the gardens of Masia Freixa. This old country house, built at the beginning of the 20th century, was designed by a modernist painter who had set up his home in the town.

3, 4, 5. The legend has it that Jupiter abandoned his wife when he met Tarragona, with whom he fell in love. The Romans formed a settlement here in 218 A.C. and the splendour of this epoch is still conserved today in the architectural remains. The city wall (4), the *forum*, the amphitheatre (5), the aqueduct, Scipio's tower and Barà's arch (3) can still be admired.

6. The first religious settlement on Montserrat was in the 11th century. Since then, the basilica has been restored several times. It contains a 12th century Romanesque carving of the Moreneta, the patron saint of Catalonia.

7. The monastery of Sant Cugat was erected on site of the old Castro Octavio, the Roman fortress that protected the settlement. Its impressive rose window has lent its name to almond sweets that are manufactured in the town, *rosetons del monestir*.

8. The impeccably conserved Cardona castle dates from the 10th century and has all the typical features of Romanesque Catalan architecture. It is hardly surprising that Orson Welles chose it as the location for one of his films.

9

9, 10. The magnificent setting of Sitges on the coast explains why many artists and intellectuals decided to set up their home there, turning the town into an important cultural hub. One of the attractions is to visit Santiago Rusiñol's "Cau Ferrat" where the famous Modernist parties were held. In addition, the town offers great beaches, harbours and a festive atmosphere at night.

10

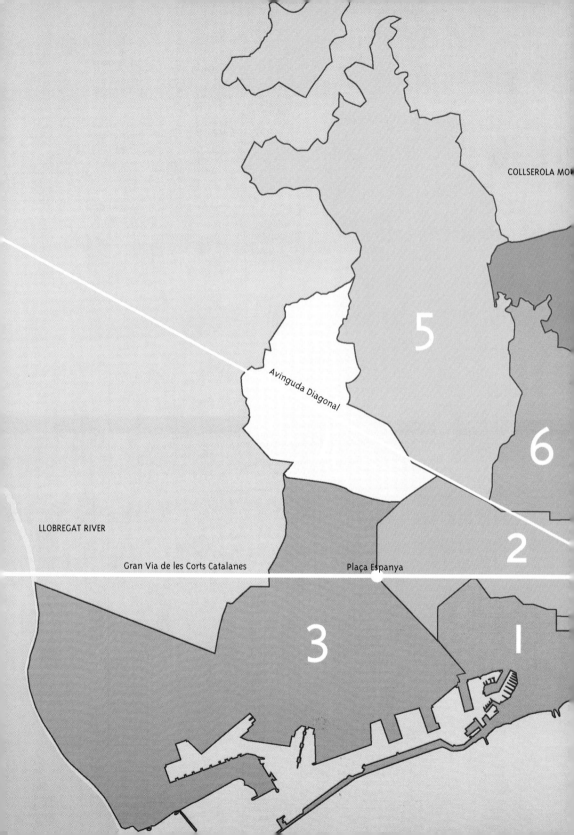

COLLSEROLA MO⬤

5

6

Avinguda Diagonal

LLOBREGAT RIVER

Gran Via de les Corts Catalanes

Plaça Espanya

2

3

1

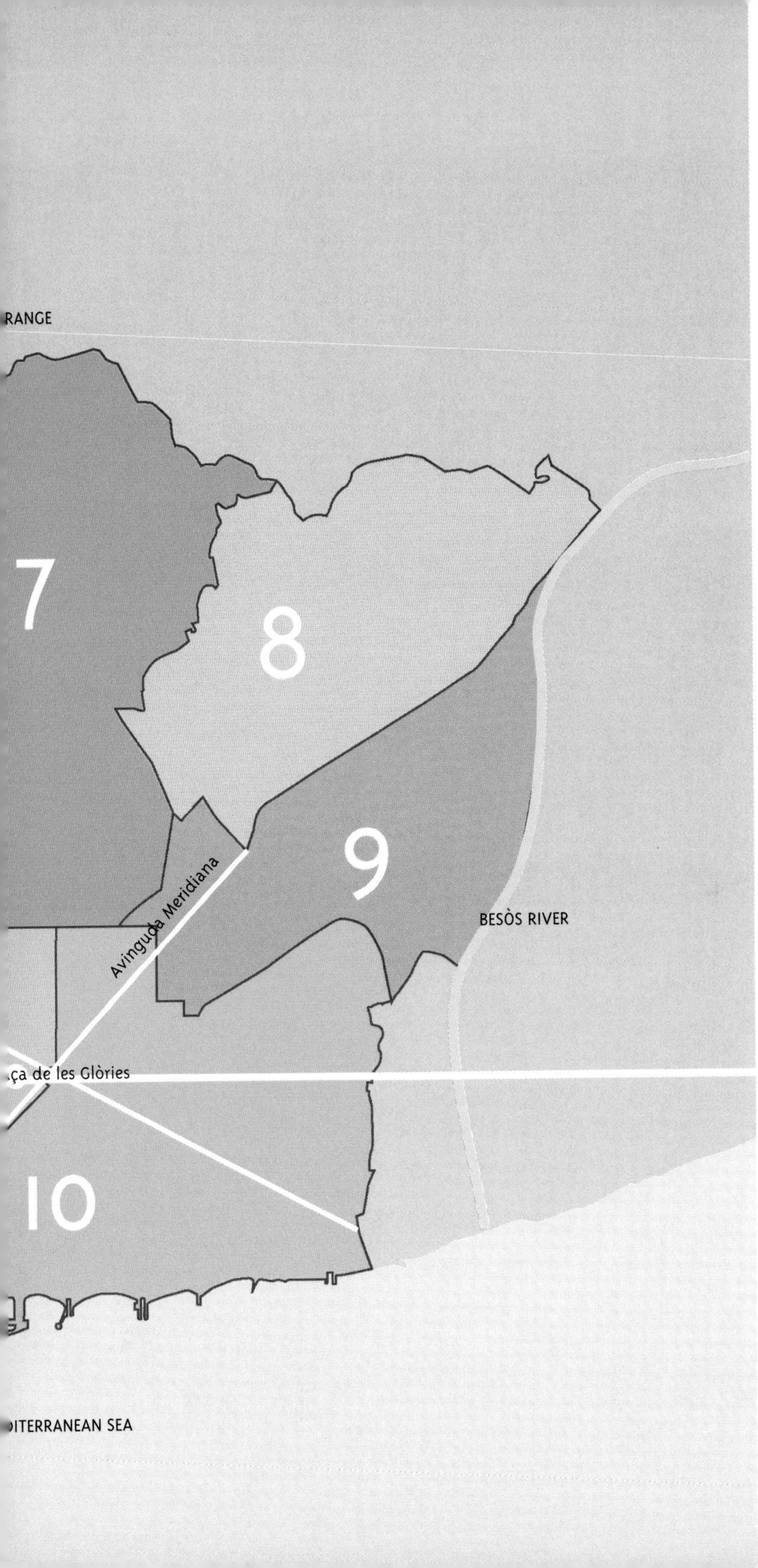

RANGE
7
8
9
Avinguda Meridiana
BESÒS RIVER
ça de les Glòries
10
ITERRANEAN SEA

Districts map

1. Ciutat Vella
2. Eixample
3. Sants-Montjuïc
4. Les Corts
5. Sarrià-Sant Gervasi
6. Gràcia
7. Horta-Guinardó
8. Nou Barris
9. Sant Andreu
10. Sant Martí

Below is a list of numbered locations, each number corresponding to the district in wich they are located, illustrated in the map on the previous page.

MUSEUMS

1. **Centre de Cultura Contemporània de Barcelona (CCCB).** Montalegre, 5. ☎ 933 064 100. ⏲tue., thu. and fri. from 11 a.m.to 2 p.m. and from 4 p.m. to 8 p.m.; wed. and sat. from 11 a.m. to 8 p.m; sun. and holidays from 11 a.m. to 7 p.m.
2. **Fundació Antoni Tàpies.** Aragó, 255. ☎ 934 870 315. ⏲tue. to sun. from 10 a.m. to 8 p.m.
3. **Fundació Joan Miró.** Avinguda Miramar, 71. ☎ 933 291 908. ⏲tue. to sat. from 10 a.m. to 7 p.m.; sun. and holidays from 10 a.m. to 2 p.m.
1. **Museu d'Art Contemporani de Barcelona (Macba).** Plaça dels Àngels, 1. ☎ 934 120 810. ⏲mon. a fri., except tue., from 11 a.m. to 7.30 p.m.; sun. and holidays from 10 a.m. to 3 p.m.
1. **Museu d'Art Modern.** Parc de la Ciutadella, s/n. ☎ 933 195 728. ⏲tue. to sat. from 10 a.m. to 7 p.m.; sun. and holidays from 10 a.m. to 2 p.m.
1. **Museu d'Història de Catalunya.** Plaça Pau Vila, 3 (Palau de Mar). ☎ 932 254 700. ⏲tue. to sat. from 10 a.m. to 7 p.m.; sun. and holidays from 10 a.m. to 14.30 p.m.
1. **Museu d'Història de la Ciutat.** Plaça del Rei, s/n. ☎ 933 151 111. ⏲tue. to sat. from 10 a.m. to 2 p.m. and from 4 p.m. to 8 p.m.; sun. and holidays from 10 a.m. to 2 p.m. Admission includes a visit to the Mirador de Martí l'Humà and Palau Reial Major del Tinell.
1. **Museu de Cera.** Passatge de la Banca, 7. ☎ 933 174 304. ⏲mon. to fri. from 10 a.m.to 1.30 p.m., and sat., sun. and holidays from 11 a 8 p.m.
5. **Museu de la Ciència.** Teodor Roviralta, 55. ☎ 932 126 050. ⏲tue. to sun. from 10 a.m. to 8 p.m.
1. **Museu Marítim.** Avinguda Drassanes, s/n. ☎ 934 541 600. ⏲mon. to fri. from 10 a.m.7 p.m.
3. **Museu Nacional d'Art de Catalunya (MNAC).** Mirador del Palau, 6. ☎ 934 237 199. ⏲tue. to sat. from 10 a.m. to 7 p.m.; sun. and holidays from 10 a.m. to 2.30 p.m.
1. **Museu Picasso.** Montcada, 15-19. ☎ 933 196 310. ⏲mon. to sat. and holidays from 10 a.m. to 8 p.m.; sun. from 10 a.m. to 3 p.m.
2. **Ruta del Modernismo.** Information centre: Passeig de Gràcia, 41. ☎ 934 880 139.

MONUMENTS

1. **Acadèmia de les Bones Lletres.** Bisbe Caçador, 3. ☎ 931 102 349.
1. **Archivo de la Corona de Aragón.** Comtes, 2. ☎ 934 854 285. ⏲mon., wed. and fri. from 9 a.m. to 6 p.m.; tue., thu. and sat. from 9 to 2 p.m.
1. **Capilla de Santa Àgata.** See Museu d'Història de la Ciutat.
2. **Casa Amatller.** See Ruta del Modernismo.
2. **Casa Batlló.** See Ruta del Modernismo.
1. **Casa de l'Ardiaca.** Santa Llúcia, 1. ☎ 933 181 195. ⏲mon. to fri. from 9 a.m. to 8.30 p.m.; sat. from 9 a.m. to 1 p.m.
1. **Casa dels Canonges.** Pietat, 2-6.
2. **Casa Milà, la Pedrera.** See Ruta del Modernismo.
3. **Castell de Montjuïc.** Carretera de Montjuïc, 66. ⏲from 7 a.m. to 10 p.m.
1. **Catedral de Barcelona.** Plaça de la Seu. ☎ 933 151 554. ⏲from 8 a.m. to 1.30 p.m. and from 17 p.m. to 7.30 p.m.
2. **Hospital de Sant Pau.** Ver Ruta del Modernismo.
1. **Iglesia de Santa Maria del Mar.** Montcada, 1. ☎ 933 102 390. ⏲from 9 a 13.30 h and from 16.30 a 20 h.
1. **Iglesia de Santa Maria del Pi.** Plaça del Pi. ☎ 933 184 743. ⏲from 9 a 13 h and from 17 a 20.30 h.
1. **Mirador de Martí l'Humà.** See Museu d'Història de la Ciutat.
4. **Monastir de Pedralbes.** Baixada Monastir, 9. Visit included in the admission to the Museu d'Història de la Ciutat.
1. **Monumento a Colón.** Portal de la Pau, 1. ☎ 933 025 224. ⏲9 a.m. to 8.30 p.m.
3. **Pabellón Mies Van der Rohe.** Avinguda Marquès de Comillas, 7. ☎ 934 234 016. ⏲10 a.m. to 8 p.m.
1. **Palau Centelles.** Baixada de Sant Miquel, 6-8.
1. **Palau de la Generalitat.** Plaça Sant Jaume. ☎ 934 024 600. ⏲from 10.30 a.m. to 1.30 p.m.on second and fourth sunday of every month.
1. **Palau del Lloctinent.** See Archivo de la Corona de Aragón.
1. **Palau Moixó.** Baixada del Caçador, 4.
1. **Palau Reial Major.** See Museu d'Història de la Ciutat.
1. **Pati Llimona.** Regomir, 3. ☎ 932 684 700. ⏲mon. to fri. from 9 a.m. to 9 p.m.; sat., sun. and holidays from 10 a.m.to 2 p.m.
2. **Sagrada Familia.** See Ruta del Modernismo.

LEISURE AND ENTERTAINMENT

1. **Aquàrium.** Moll d'Espanya, s/n. ☎ 932 217 474. ⏲winter: from 9 a.m. to 9 p.m.; summer: from 9 a.m. to 11 p.m.
10. **Casino de Barcelona.** Marina, 19-21. ☎ 932 257 878. ⏲1 p.m. to 5 a.m.
1. **Globus Turístic.** Passeig de Circunvalació. ☎ 906 301 282. ⏲mon. to thu. from 10.30 a.m. to 7p.m.; fri. to sun. from 10.30 a.m. to 9 p.m.

1. **Golondrinas.** Portal de la Pau, s/n. ☎ 934 423 106. ⊙winter: mon. to fri. from 11 a.m. to 2 p.m., holidays from 11.45 a.m. to 5 p.m.; summer: mon. to fri. from 11 a.m. to 7 p.m., holidays from 11.45 a.m. to 7 p.m.
5. **Mirador Torre de Collserola.** Carretera de Vallvidrera al Tibidabo. ☎ 934 069 354. ⊙ wed., thu. and fri. from 11.00 a.m. to 2.30 p.m. and from 2.30 p.m. to 6.00 p.m.; sat., sun. and holidays from 11.00 a.m. to 7.00 p.m.
5. **Parc d'Atracciones del Tibidabo.** Plaça del Tibidabo, 3. ☎ 932 117 942. ⊙sat., sun. and holidays; winter: from 12 p.m. to 6 p.m.; summer: from 12 p.m. to 9 p.m.
3. **Poble Espanyol.** Avinguda Marquès de Comillas, 25. ☎ 935 086 300. ⊙mon. from 9 a.m. to 8 p.m.; tue. to thu. from 9 a.m. to 2 a.m.; fri. and sat. from 9 a.m. to 4 a.m.; sun. and holidays from 9 a.m. to 24 p.m.
1. **Telefèric de Montjuïc.** H 11 a.m. to 7.15 p.m.
5.**Tramvia Blau.** Tour starts from Plaça Kennedy. ⊙saturdays, sundays and local holidays between 10 a.m. and 9 p.m. every 15 minutes.
1. **Zoo de Barcelona.** Parc de la Ciutadella. ☎ 932 256 780. ⊙november to february from 10 a.m. to 5 p.m.; may to august from 9.30 a.m. to 7.30 p.m.; march and october from 10 a.m. to 6 p.m., and april and september from 10 a.m. to 7 p.m.

BARS AND CLUBS

1. **Abaixadors Deu.** Abaixadors, 10. ⊙18 p.m. to 3 a.m.; fri. and sat. until 4 a.m.
10. **Baja Beach Club.** Passeig Marítim de la Barceloneta, s/n. H thu. a sun. hasta las 5 h.
10. **Be Good.** Sancho de Ávila, 78.
10. **Bóveda.** Pallars, 97.
6. **Café del Sol.** Plaça del Sol, 16. ⊙ 1 p.m. to 3 a.m.
1. **Cafetería Zurich.** Pelai, 39 (next to Plaça Catalunya). ⊙8 p.m. to 1 a.m.
1. **Glaciar.** Plaça Reial, 3. ⊙16 p.m. to 2.30 a.m.; sun. from 8 a.m. to 2.15 p.m.
1. **Jamboree.** Plaça Reial, 17. ⊙9 p.m. to 5 a.m.
10. **L'Ovella Negra.** Zamora, 78.
1. **La Macarena.** Nou de Sant Francesc, 5. ⊙11 p.m. to 4 a.m.; fri. and sat. until 5.30 a.m.
1. **Maremàgnum.** Moll d'Espanya, s/n. ⊙until 5 a.m.
2. **Mediterráneo.** Balmes, 129.
5. **Mirablau.** Plaça Doctor Andreu, s/n. ⊙11 a.m. to 4.30 a.m.
1. **Miramelindo.** Passeig del Born, 15. ⊙8 p.m. to 2.30 a.m.; fri. and sat. until 3.30 a.m.
2. **Nick Havana.** Rosselló, 208. ⊙11 p.m. to 5 a.m. from thu. to fri.
10. **Port Olímpic.** Ronda Litoral Mar. ⊙until 5 a.m.
10. **Razzmatazz.** Almogàvers, 122. ⊙11 p.m. to 5 a.m. thu. to sat.
5. **Rosebud.** Adrià Margarit, 17. ⊙9 p.m. to 5 a.m.
6. **Sol Soler.** Plaça del Sol, 13. ⊙7 p.m. to 2.30 a.m.
5. **Universal.** Marià Cubí, 184. ⊙10 p.m. to 3.30 a.m.; fri. and sat. until 4.30 a.m.
2. **Velvet.** Balmes, 161. ⊙10 p.m. to 5 a.m. from thu. to sun.

RESTAURANTS

1. **Agua.** Passeig Marítim de la Barceloneta, 30 (Marina Village).☎ 932 251 272. ⊙1.30 p.m. to 4.30 p.m. and 8.30 p.m. to 24 p.m.
6. **Café Salambó.** Torrijos, 51. ☎ 932 186 966. ⊙1 p.m. to 4 a.m. and 9 p.m. to 1 a.m.
5. **El Bristot de Bruno.** Oliana, 14. T 932 016 369. ⊙1 p.m. to 3.30 p.m. and 9 p.m. to 2 a.m. Sat. and sun. only at night.
1. **Fresc Co.** València, 263. ☎. 934 881 049. ⊙1 p.m. to 5 a.m. and from 8 p.m. to 1 a.m. Rambla Universitat, 29. ☎ 933 016 937.
2. **La Flauta.** Aribau, 23. ☎ 933 237 038. ⊙7.30 a.m. to 1.30 a.m. Closed sat. and sund. local holidays.
2. **La Provença.** Provença, 242. ☎ 933 232 367. ⊙1.30 p.m. to 3.30 p.m. and 9 p.m. to 11.30 p.m.
5. **La Vaqueria.** Deu i Mata, 141. ☎ 934 190 735. ⊙1.30 p.m. to 4 p.m. and 9 p.m. to 24 p.m. Sat. and sun. only at night.
6. **La Torreta de Gràcia.** Verdi, 179-181. ☎ 932 370 268. ⊙1 p.m. to 4 p.m. and 8.30 p.m. to 24 p.m.
1. **Euskal Etxea.** Placeta Montcada, 1-3. ☎ 933 102 185. ⊙12.30 p.m. to 3.30 p.m. and 7.30 p.m. to 11.30 p.m. Closed mon. and sun. night.
1. **Pou Dols.** Baixada de Sant Miquel, 6. ☎ 934 120 579. ⊙1.30 p.m. to 4 p.m. and 9 p.m. to 24 p.m. Sunday closed.
10. **Rabasseda.** Plaça Mercadal, 1. ☎ 933 451 017. ⊙1 p.m. to 4 p.m. and 9 p.m. to 11 p.m. Sunday and Monday closed.
2. **Semproniana.** Rosselló, 148. ☎ 934 531 820. ⊙1.30 p.m. to 4 p.m. and 9 p.m. to 11.30 p.m. Sunday closed.
1. **Senyor Parellada.** Argenteria, 37. ☎ 933 105 094. ⊙1 p.m. to 3.30 p.m. and 9 p.m. to 11.30 p.m. Sunday closed.
10. **Teatre Nacional de Catalunya.** Plaça de les Arts, 1. ☎ 933 065 729. ⊙8 p.m. to 2 a.m. Sunday and Monday closed.

PARKS

All public parks open at 10 a.m. Closing hours vary depending on the time of year: from November to February, until 6 p.m.; March and October, until 7 p.m.; April and September, until 8 p.m., and from May to August, until 9 p.m.

INDEX

RECOMMENDED BIBLIOGRAPHY

AMELANG J.S., GIL X. y MCDONOGH G.W. **Doce paseos por la historia de Barcelona.**
Ajuntament de Barcelona, 1992.

AROCA M.V. and VILLALONGA I. **Barcelona a 100. Protagonistas de una nueva generación.**
Ed. Sirpus. Barcelona, 1997.

CARLAS M. **Cena conmigo esta noche.**
Ed. Plaza&Janés. Barcelona, 1999.

CIRICI A. **Barcelona pam a pam.**
Ed. Teide. Barcelona, 1986.

DEMORY M.A. **Un gran fin de semana en Barcelona.**
Ed. Salvat. Barcelona, 2000.

HUERTAS J.M. and ENCINAS P. **50 veces Barcelona.**
Ajuntament de Barcelona, 2000.

HUGHES R. **Barcelona.**
Ed. Anagrama. Barcelona, 1992.

VAN ZANDT L. **La vida y obras Gaudí.**
Ed. Kliczkowski Publisher/Asppan CP67. Madrid, 1997.

VILLALONGA I. **Restaurantes de Barcelona.**
Ed. Òptima. Barcelona, 1999.

VILLALONGA I. **Bares de Barcelona.**
Ed. Òptima. Barcelona, 2000.

Gaudí y la Ruta del Modernismo.
Ed. Kliczkowski Publisher-A Asppan SL. Barcelona, 2001.

Guía del ocio.
A city guide that is published weekly and goes on sale on Fridays.